Family Bible Study

THE
Herschel
HOBBS
COMMENTARY®

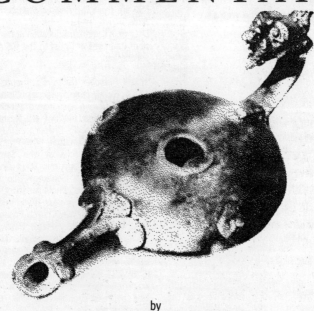

by

Robert J. Dean

SUMMER 2004
Volume 4, Number 4

GENE MIMS, *President*
LifeWay Church Resources

Ross H. McLaren
Editor in Chief

Carolyn Gregory
Copy Editor

Stephen Smith
Graphic Designer

Frankie Churchwell
Technical Specialist

Michael Felder
Lead Adult Ministry Specialist

John McClendon
Mic Morrow
Adult Ministry Specialists

Send questions/comments to
  Editor, Herschel Hobbs Commentary
One LifeWay Plaza
Nashville, TN 37234-0175
Or make comments on the web at
www.lifeway.com

Management Personnel

Louis B. Hanks, *Director*
Publishing
Gary Hauk, *Director*
Leadership and Adult Publishing
Ron Brown, Bill Craig, *Managing Directors*
Leadership and Adult Publishing
Alan Raughton, *Director*
Church Strategies

The Herschel Hobbs Commentary (ISSN 0191-4219), *Family Bible Study*, is published quarterly by LifeWay Christian Resources of the Southern Baptist Convention, One LifeWay Plaza, Nashville, Tennessee 37234; James T. Draper, Jr., President, and Ted Warren, Executive Vice-President, LifeWay Christian Resources of the Southern Baptist Convention; © Copyright 2004 LifeWay Christian Resources of the Southern Baptist Convention. All rights reserved. Single subscription to individual address, $20.95 per year. If you need help with an order, WRITE LifeWay Church Resources Customer Service, One LifeWay Plaza, Nashville, Tennessee 37234-0113; For subscriptions, FAX (615) 251-5818 or EMAIL subscribe@lifeway.com. For bulk shipments mailed quarterly to one address, FAX (615) 251-5933 or EMAIL CustomerService@lifeway.com. Order ONLINE at www.lifeway.com. Mail address changes to: *The Herschel Hobbs Commentary, Family Bible Study,* One LifeWay Plaza, Nashville, TN 37234-0113.

Printed in the United States of America.

Dedicated to the Memory of

Martha Myers

William Koehn

Kathy Gariety

Missionaries to Yemen

Killed on December 30, 2002

"This [gunman] did not take their lives;

they chose to give their lives long ago when they responded

to God's call."

(John Brady, International Mission Board)

Contents

Study Theme

Body Life 6

That's Encouraging! 46

Contents

Peter's Principles for Successful Living   87

Study Theme

Body Life

"You have a reputation for being alive, but you are dead" (Rev. 3:1, HCSB). The living Lord Jesus had John to write these words to the church at Sardis. What a terrible epitaph for a church!

What is the difference between a dead church and a living one? This study on "Body Life" focuses on churches that are filled with life. These are churches that follow Christ as Head of His body, the church. The members of such churches see the church not as a convenience for them but as a channel of commitment through which to do their part in the life of the body of Christ.

This study focuses on four aspects of body life in the church: baptism, the Lord's Supper, church leadership, and spiritual gifts. Each of these areas magnifies Christ.

The first lesson, "Baptism," is based on Acts 2:36-41 and Romans 6:1-10. This lesson shows why Baptists practice believers' baptism by immersion. Christ is magnified by the depiction of death, burial, and resurrection: His own, the spiritual resurrection to walk in new life, and the future resurrection.

The second lesson, "The Lord's Supper," is based on Matthew 26:26-29, when Jesus instituted this ordinance, and 1 Corinthians 11:23-32, when Paul instructed the Corinthians in its meaning.

The third lesson, "Church Leadership," is based on passages from 1 Timothy and Hebrews. These passages deal with what leaders and members should be to enable all to follow Christ.

The fourth lesson, "Spiritual Gifts," is based on verses from 1 Corinthians 12. The body of Christ is one but has a variety of gifts. These are to be used for the glory of God and the good of the church as a whole.

This study theme is designed to help you:
- appreciate the importance of baptism in the Christian life (June 6)
- consistently partake of the Lord's Supper in a manner worthy of Christ (June 13)
- support and submit to godly church leaders (June 20)
- discover and exercise your spiritual gift (June 27)

BAPTISM

Bible Passages: Acts 2:36-41; Romans 6:1-10
Key Verse: Acts 2:38

❖ *Significance of the Lesson*

• The *Theme* of this lesson is that all Christians need to be baptized as an act of obedience to the Lord Jesus Christ.
• The *Life Question* this lesson addresses is, What makes baptism so important?
• The *Biblical Truth* is that Christians demonstrate their obedience to Christ and identification with Him by being baptized.
• The *Life Impact* is to help you appreciate the importance of baptism in the Christian life.

Attitudes Toward Baptism

Christians are exposed to a variety of attitudes toward baptism. The secular mind largely ignores baptism as a meaningless religious ritual. Some people are trusting in their baptism as their ticket to heaven. Some churchgoers and professed believers have never been baptized. Many people are confused by the differences about baptism among Christian denominations.

Christian denominations have differences about baptism. There are differences about the *how, who,* and *why* of baptism. The modes of baptism range all the way from sprinkling to immersion. The people to be baptized range from infants to older adults and from the uncommitted to believers. The purpose of baptism is defined by some denominations as the forgiveness of sins, but others deny that the waters of baptism wash away sins.

Baptists hold to believers' baptism by immersion. That is, we believe that immersion was how new believers were baptized according to the New Testament. Only immersion depicts death, burial, and resurrection. Because Baptists believe in a regenerate church membership, we believe that only believers are to be baptized. The purpose of baptism is not to save or contribute to salvation. The purpose is to obey Christ by openly identifying oneself with Christ and His church.

Word Study: *Baptized*

The English word *baptized* is a transliteration, not a translation of the Greek word *baptizo*. The Greeks used the word to mean "immerse," "dip," or "submerge." For example, the word described a sunken ship. The Greek translation of the Old Testament used this word to describe Naaman's dipping seven times in the Jordan River (2 Kings 5:14). In the New Testament are similar examples. Luke 11:38 uses the word of washing hands by submerging them in water. Why then didn't the early translators into English use *immersed* rather than merely transliterate the Greek word? Probably they wanted to allow for differences of opinion about the mode of baptism. Few serious Bible students deny that immersion was the practice recorded in the New Testament.

❖ *Search the Scriptures*

In his sermon on the Day of Pentecost, Peter called the people to repent and be baptized. Those who received his word were baptized. Baptism pictures death and resurrection.

The three outline points answer the Life Question.

An Act of Obedience (Acts 2:36-41)

Why do Baptists believe that Acts 2:38 does not teach that baptism secures forgiveness of sins? What is the purpose of being baptized? Why do we believe in believer's baptism by immersion?

Acts 2:36-38: Therefore let all the house of Israel know assuredly, that God hath made that same Jesus, whom ye have crucified, both Lord and Christ. [37] Now when they heard this, they were pricked in their heart, and said unto Peter and to the rest of the apostles, Men and brethren, what shall we do? [38] Then Peter said unto them, Repent, and be baptized everyone of you in the name of Jesus Christ for the remission of sins, and ye shall receive the gift of the Holy Ghost [Spirit].

Was there ever a day like the one described in Acts 2? The promised Holy Spirit filled the faithful 120 who had been praying. The marvelous event was marked by signs from heaven: the sound of the rushing wind, the tongues of fire, and the miracle that enabled the believers to speak in the languages of the people to whom they witnessed. When someone said that the witnesses were drunk, Peter spoke to the crowd. He quoted Joel's prediction of the age of the Spirit, and he said the people were seeing that prophecy fulfilled. Then Peter preached a powerful sermon that focused on the cross and resurrection. He accused his hearers of sharing in the guilt for crucifying Jesus.

Verse 36 brings home the crux of his message. Peter wanted them to **know assuredly** ("with certainty," HCSB) three things: (1) Jesus of Nazareth was crucified. **That same Jesus** referred back to the "man approved of God" (v. 22). (2) They shared in the guilt for condemning Jesus. Peter said that they had **crucified** Jesus. (3) God reversed this false condemnation by raising Jesus from the dead, thus showing Him to be **both Lord and Christ.** He was the promised Messiah and the divine Lord (see Phil. 2:9-11).

Peter's hearers were **pricked in their heart** ("pierced to the heart," HCSB; "cut to the heart," NIV). The word of God through Peter and the other Spirit-filled witnesses convicted the people of their guilt in crucifying the Lord and Christ. They asked Peter and the others, **What shall we do?**

Verse 38 is the heart of Peter's answer to their question. It is a key verse for many reasons. It contains four components: **repent . . . be baptized . . . remission** ("forgiveness," NIV, HCSB) **of sins . . . the gift of the Holy Ghost** [Spirit]. Each of these is important, and the relationship between and among them is even more important. The main word is the call to **repent.** This was the message of the Old Testament prophets, John the Baptist, Jesus, and the apostles. This is the first thing that a convicted sinner must do. The word means "to turn." Repentance grows out of conviction and includes godly sorrow, but it is basically turning from sin. Sinners may be convicted and sorry, but they do not repent until they turn from their sin. Those who truly repent by turning from their sins also believe in Christ by turning to God. Sometimes in the Book of Acts, both repentance and faith are mentioned (20:21). At times only repentance is mentioned (17:30) or only faith (16:31), but the use of one assumes the other.

What is the relationship between repentance and baptism? Some people assume that this verse teaches that both repentance and baptism are necessary in order for sins to be forgiven. They take **for** to mean "in order to receive." Herschel H. Hobbs, who studied Greek under A. T. Robertson, wrote of another way to translate the Greek preposition *eis:* "A. T. Robertson, the leading Greek scholar of the twentieth century, said that this preposition should be translated in Acts 2:38 as at, because of, on the basis of, or as a result of. In Luke 11:32 exactly the same usage of *eis* is translated: 'For they [Nineveh] repented *at* the preaching of Jonas' (author's italics). The people of Nineveh repented not for, into, or in order that Jonah might preach, but as the result of his preaching. So Peter said, in effect, 'Repent and be baptized as the result of or on the basis of the remission of sins.' This translation fits exactly the broad teaching of the New Testament."[1]

After mentioning this point, John B. Polhill wrote of another reason not to see baptismal regeneration in verse 38: "The usual connection of the forgiveness of sins in Luke-Acts is with repentance and not with baptism at all (cf. Luke 24:47; Acts 3:19; 5:31). In fact, in no other passage of Acts is baptism presented as bringing about the forgiveness of sins. If not linked with repentance, forgiveness is connected with faith (cf. 10:43; 13:38f.; 26:18)."[2] Our view of baptism is closely linked with our view of salvation. We believe that the Bible presents salvation as by grace through faith, not by any good works or religious acts that we do.

If someone asked, "What must I do to be saved?" a saved person might say something like this: "You need to repent by turning from your sins and you need to turn to God by placing your faith in Jesus Christ as your Savior." If someone asked, "What should I do?" a saved person might say something like this: "First you need to be saved by turning from sin and trusting Jesus as your Savior. Then you need to be baptized and become an active member of a church." If someone replied, "Why should I be baptized if it is not necessary for me to be saved?" a Christian might say something like this: "A truly saved person wants to obey Christ as Lord. Baptism is an act of obedience that sets the tone for a life of obedience." Other reasons for being baptized will be identified later in the lesson comments.

The gift of the Holy Ghost [Spirit] is also the result of becoming a Christian. He comes into our hearts when we first believe (Rom. 8:9), and we need to yield ourselves daily to Him and be filled with Him (Eph. 5:18). Although being baptized is not when the Spirit first enters a believer's life, baptism—like every act of obedience to Christ—should result in a fresh anointing of the Spirit's presence.

Acts 2:39-41: **For the promise is unto you, and to your children, and to all that are afar off, even as many as the Lord our God shall call. [40]And with many other words did he testify and exhort, saying, Save yourselves from this untoward generation. [41]Then they that gladly received his word were baptized: and the same day there were added unto them about three thousand souls.**

Verse 39 is part of Peter's answer to the crowd's question in verse 37. **The promise** is the promise of forgiveness of sins and the gift of the Spirit in verse 38. Peter told them that this promise was not only for them but also for their **children, and to all that are afar off, even as many as the Lord our God shall call.** Their **children** refers not just to their sons and daughters but also to their descendants into the future. Some supporters of infant baptism have used this verse to bolster their position, but this does not seem to have been Peter's meaning (see comments on v. 41). **All that are afar off** refers to people in places other than there. Most of the group on that day probably thought of fellow Jews scattered all over the civilized world, but perhaps some remembered the Lord's Great Commission. By the end of the Book of Acts, the gospel was being proclaimed to Gentiles, and many believed.

Peter continued to testify and exhort them **with many other words.** The gist of his words was the urgent invitation: **Save yourselves from this untoward** ("corrupt," NIV, HCSB) **generation.** "His reference to a 'corrupt generation' (*skolias*, 'crooked,' perverse') is Old Testament language for a generation that is stubborn and rebellious and not faithful to God (Ps. 78:8; cf. Deut. 32:5; Phil. 2:15). The Jews at Pentecost were part of such a generation, a generation that witnessed the coming of the Messiah and rejected him."[3] The plea **save yourselves** at first sounds as if sinners participate in their own salvation, but that is true only to the degree that we either receive or reject the salvation offered by God. Imagine that a ship sank and survivors were trying to keep from drowning. Then a rescue vessel arrived and threw out lifelines to the drowning people. Only the lifelines offered salvation from drowning. But someone on the rescue ship might call out, "Save yourselves. Grab one of the lifelines."

Verse 41 is another key verse in the doctrine and practice of Christian baptism. Many who heard Peter's message **gladly received his**

word. Gladly received translates *apodechomai*. When this word is used of people, it means "to welcome or receive someone favorably." Acts 28:30 tells how Paul "welcomed" (NIV, HCSB) all who came to visit him in his confinement in Rome. In the same way, many gladly received the word. Their first reaction to Peter's message left them deeply disturbed because of their sins. But after hearing the good news of forgiveness of sins, they welcomed this wonderful promise and claimed it as their own. Gladly receiving the message means that they repented of their sins and committed themselves to Jesus. **About three thousand** of them welcomed the good news and **were baptized.**

This is the first example of what is called "believers' baptism." This means two things: (1) Only believers were baptized. (2) All believers were baptized. This is the consistent pattern throughout the Book of Acts (8:28-40; 16:14-15,30-34).

Although Baptists insist that baptism does not wash away sins or secure forgiveness or salvation, we consider this church ordinance to be very important. Because it is one of the first acts of obedience to the Lord, baptism should be a deep and meaningful experience for the person being baptized and a cause for rejoicing for those who witness the baptism.

What are the lasting lessons in Acts 2:36-41?

1. The preaching of the gospel brings conviction to sinners and provides the promise of forgiveness to those who repent and believe.

2. Baptism does not forgive sins, but is an act of obedience to the Lord.

3. Baptists believe the New Testament teaches that only believers are baptized and that all believers are to be baptized.

A Symbol of Death (Rom. 6:1-3)

*How can one dead in sin become **dead to sin**? How are people **baptized into Jesus Christ**? How are they **baptized into his death**?*

Romans 6:1-3: What shall we say then? Shall we continue in sin, that grace may abound? [2]God forbid. How shall we, that are dead to sin, live any longer therein? [3]Know ye not, that so many of us as were baptized into Jesus Christ were baptized into his death?

Romans 6 is closely tied to the end of chapter 5. Paul showed how Adam brought sin and death into the world, but God's grace in Jesus reversed that process by bringing salvation from sin and eternal life

(5:12-21). Paul wrote, "Where sin abounded, grace did much more abound" (v. 20).

The opponents of grace asked, **Shall we continue in sin, that grace may abound?** This was a mocking question. They said that if grace abounds where sin abounds, should we not sin more in order to receive more grace? Their question revealed how little they knew of God's grace. Paul reacted strongly to this distorted view of grace. He wrote, **God forbid** ("Absolutely not!" HCSB; "By no means!" NIV). He asked a question of these enemies of grace, **How shall we, that are dead to sin** ("who died to sin," HCSB), **live any longer therein?**

Paul elsewhere referred to those without Christ as "dead in trespasses and sins" (Eph. 2:1). Here he wrote of those who have died to sin. The dead no longer participate in the activities of the living. People who are dead *in* sin do not know God and spiritual realities. When people become Christians, they die *to* sin. They are dead to the old life of sin. They no longer participate in the life of sin. Notice that Paul was writing in verse 2 about not living a sinful life. Other passages show that Christians continue to struggle with temptation, sometimes fail, and need to pray for forgiveness for occasional sins. Paul's point here is that Christians do not **live** in sin.

The reason for this change is that as **many of us as were baptized into Jesus Christ were baptized into his death.** There are three main interpretations of these words as far as baptism is concerned. Some people believe these words have nothing to do with water baptism. According to this view, the word **baptized** is used of our spiritual immersion in Christ. The second view goes to the other extreme and identifies water baptism as the way people experience the benefits of Christ's death for them. Many hold a third view. The time when we receive Christ is when He comes into our hearts and when we come to be in Him. Baptism in water symbolizes the cleansing of sins and the power to overcome sin's power.

Being **baptized into** Christ's **death** is what Paul meant by being crucified with Christ (Gal. 2:20). He did not mean that we go back to Calvary but that the crucified Lord brings Calvary to us. The cross is the door to the Christian life because Christ died for our sins and God saves us from sin's penalty when we trust Christ. The cross then becomes the way of Christian living. Through the presence of the crucified Lord, He enables us to deny ourselves, take up our cross, and follow Him. It is unthinkable that anyone who claims to follow Him would continue to live in sin.

What are some lasting lessons in Romans 6:1-3?

1. Faith in Christ involves a personal union with Jesus Christ.

2. The cross is not only the door to the Christian life but also the way of this life.

3. Sinners who were dead in sin become dead to sin through their union with Christ and being crucified with Christ.

4. Water baptism symbolizes the death of Christ and our death to sin through Him.

A Symbol of Life (Rom. 6:4-10)

How does verse 4 complete the message of verse 3? What three realities of death and resurrection are depicted in baptism? How does Christ break the domination of sin and death?

Romans 6:4-10: Therefore we are buried with him by baptism into death: that like as Christ was raised up from the dead by the glory of the Father, even so we also should walk in newness of life. [5]For if we have been planted together in the likeness of his death, we shall be also in the likeness of his resurrection: [6]Knowing this, that our old man is crucified with him, that the body of sin might be destroyed, that henceforth we should not serve sin. [7]For he that is dead is freed from sin. [8]Now if we be dead with Christ, we believe that we shall also live with him: [9]knowing that Christ being raised from the dead dieth no more; death hath no more dominion over him. [10]For in that he died, he died unto sin once: but in that he liveth, he liveth unto God.

Baptism pictures not only death and burial but also resurrection. Verse 3 pointed to death; verse 4 adds the picture of resurrection from the dead. Baptism by immersion points to three deaths, burials, and resurrections. "In baptism . . . the believer symbolizes Jesus' death, burial, and resurrection; the death of the believer to sin, his burial, and resurrection to walk in a new life in Christ; and his faith in the final resurrection from the dead."[4] The atoning death of Jesus and His resurrection from the dead are inseparable parts of the gospel message (1 Cor. 15:3-4) and also of our Christian experience. The first part of Romans 6:4 repeats the emphasis on death and burial from verse 3, but quickly ties it to being raised from the dead. Verse 3 stressed that we can no longer live in sin because in Christ we have died to sin. The opposite of living in sin is living a new life. Christians no longer live in sin because **we are buried with him by baptism into death.**

We **walk in newness of life** because we have within us the presence and power of **Christ** who **was raised up from the dead by the glory of the Father.** "New life in Christ follows death to sin as certainly as Christ's resurrection followed his crucifixion."[5] Paul was not teaching that the death and resurrection of Jesus provide only an example we can follow. Only the presence and power of Christ within us makes possible living in newness of life.

This is supported by the repetition of the Greek word *sun*, which means "with" or "together with." This appears as a preposition and as a prefix to a verb. Several of these are found in Romans 6:4-8: **buried with him . . . planted together** ("joined with," HCSB; "united with," NIV) . . . **crucified with him . . . dead with Christ . . . live with him.** These show that the nature of salvation and Christian living involves union with Jesus Christ. This union with the crucified and risen Lord empowers believers to die to sin and live a new life.

Paul, like Jesus (John 8:34), saw sin as a power that enslaves its victims in a plight from which they cannot save themselves. The word **serve** is the Greek word for serving as a slave. The word **freed** describes freedom from sin's slavery. Only the presence and power of Christ within can deliver us from the slavery of sin. Today is the 60th anniversary of D-Day in World War II. At great cost, the Allied forces won a decisive victory over the Nazi power that had dominated and enslaved most of continental Europe. In a sense, D-Day ensured VE-Day. Many died before the final victory, but the domination of the Nazis was ended. In a far more wondrous way the death and resurrection of Jesus ended the domination of sin and death over humanity.

Verse 9 declares the uniqueness of Christ's resurrection from the dead. During His ministry, Jesus restored to life several who had died; however, each of them later died again. By contrast **Christ being raised from the dead dieth no more; death hath no more dominion over him.** Through union with the crucified and risen Lord, we partake of His victory over sin and death. We are set free from the slavery of sin and death.

What are the lasting lessons of Romans 6:4-10?

1. Dying with Christ and being raised with Him ensure not only that believers do not live in sin but also that we live new lives.

2. People apart from Christ are under the dominion of sin and death, but Christ's death and resurrection ensure for believers victory over sin and death.

3. Baptism pictures three deaths and resurrections: Christ's death and resurrection, a believer's dying to sin and being raised to new life, and the future resurrection.

❖ *Spiritual Transformations*

When Peter preached the death and resurrection at Pentecost, he called the convicted sinners to repent and be baptized. Those who gladly received his word were baptized. Paul wrote about being buried with Christ by baptism unto death and being raised up to walk in newness of life.

The New Testament teaches believers' baptism by immersion. Only believers were baptized, but all believers were baptized.

If someone said to you, "I'm a believer, but I've never been baptized," how many of the following reasons for being baptized might you use?

❑ Jesus commanded believers to be baptized.
❑ Being baptized is the biblical way of openly identifying yourself with Christ.
❑ Being baptized is the biblical way of becoming part of Christ's church.
❑ Being baptized pictures the death and resurrection of Christ, your experience of dying to sin and being raised up to newness of life, and your hope of future resurrection from the dead.

Prayer of Commitment: Lord, help me to live the new life in Christ to which I committed myself in baptism. Amen.

[1] Herschel H. Hobbs, *Fundamentals of Our Faith* [Nashville: Broadman Press, 1960], 118.

[2] John B. Polhill "Acts," in *The New American Commentary,* vol. 26 [Nashville: Broadman Press, 1992], 117.

[3] Polhill, "Acts," NAC, 118.

[4] Herschel H. Hobbs, *An Exposition of the Gospel of Matthew* [Grand Rapids: Baker Book House, 1965], 367-368.

[5] Robert H. Mounce, "Romans," in *The New American Commentary,* vol. 27 [Nashville: Broadman & Holman Publishers, 1995], 150.

THE LORD'S SUPPER

Background Passages: Matthew 26:17-30; 1 Corinthians 11:17-34
Focal Passages: Matthew 26:26-29; 1 Corinthians 11:23-32
Key Verse: 1 Corinthians 11:26

❖ *Significance of the Lesson*

• The *Theme* of this lesson is that all Christians need to understand the significance of the Lord's Supper and to partake of it on a regular basis.

• The *Life Question* this lesson addresses is, What significance does the Lord's Supper have for me and for my church?

• The *Biblical Truth* is that Christians demonstrate their love for Christ and unity with one another by partaking of the Lord's Supper together on a regular basis.

• The *Life Impact* is to help you consistently partake of the Lord's Supper in a manner worthy of Christ.

How People Think About the Lord's Supper

Secular people often see the Lord's Supper as a meaningless religious ritual. Many are confused by the denominational differences about it. Some religious people consider the Lord's Supper very important, but others fail to see its importance for them. Celebrating the Lord's Supper can become a meaningless ritual or a meaningful worship experience. Christians need to understand the meaning of the Lord's Supper and participate in it consistently and in a manner worthy of Christ.

An Ordinance of the Church

Baptists refer to baptism and the Lord's Supper as ordinances of the church. An *ordinance* is a commandment calling for obedience. The ordinances are referred to as *symbols* of great spiritual realities, and our reason to be baptized and to partake of the Lord's Supper is obedience. These two words—*symbol* and *obedience*—are most often used by Baptists to define the ordinances and why Christians should participate.

Word Study: *Unworthily*

Unworthily translates *anaxios* in 1 Corinthians 11:27. It is an adverb meaning "in an unworthy way" (HCSB), not an adjective meaning "unworthy." The adjective appears in 1 Corinthians 6:2: "Do ye not know that the saints shall judge the world? and if the world shall be judged by you, are ye unworthy to judge the smallest matters?" Paul did not say that unworthy people should not take the Lord's Supper. We are all unworthy people. He was dealing with how believers partake of the Lord's Supper.

❖ Search the Scriptures

During the Last Supper, Jesus instituted the Lord's Supper. Paul reminded the Corinthians of the meaning of the Lord's Supper. He said it provided an opportunity for self-examination.

The three outline points teach us three important lessons related to the Lord's Supper.

Instituted by Christ (Matt. 26:26-29)

*When did Jesus institute the Lord's Supper? What are the different interpretations of His words, **this is my body**? To what does **all** refer in verse 27? What is the significance of verse 29?*

Matthew 26:26-29: And as they were eating, Jesus took bread, and blessed it, and brake it, and gave it to the disciples, and said, Take, eat; this is my body. ²⁷And he took the cup, and gave thanks, and gave it to them, saying, Drink ye all of it; ²⁸for this is my blood of the new testament, which is shed for many for the remission of sins. ²⁹But I say unto you, I will not drink henceforth of this fruit of the vine, until that day when I drink it new with you in my Father's kingdom.

Jesus instituted the Lord's Supper on the night before His crucifixion. He ate supper with the twelve, who still did not understand the reason Jesus kept predicting His rejection, death, and resurrection. Luke 22:24-30 says that they were still arguing about which of them was greatest. At that meal Jesus predicted that one of them was going to betray Him. Judas, the betrayer, seems to have left before Jesus instituted the Lord's Supper.

Jesus and the apostles were eating a Passover meal together, not seated at a table as in the famous painting by Leonardo da Vinci. In the custom of that day, they reclined behind couches. The Passover feast commemorated the deliverance of Israel from Egypt. The meal helped each generation of Jews relive the events of the exodus. Jesus became our Passover Lamb by dying to deliver us from sin and death (1 Cor. 5:7). In a sense, the Lord's Supper is for Christians what the Passover was to the Jews. The institution of the Lord's Supper, in connection with an actual meal, led to the early practice of taking the Lord's Supper after a fellowship meal.

Jesus took bread, and blessed it, and brake it, and gave it to the disciples. This was not an unusual sight for the apostles. It was Jesus' custom to thank the Father for food. Before feeding the 5,000 He did this (Matt. 14:19). The two on the Emmaus Road would recognize Jesus when "he took bread, and blessed it, and brake it, and gave to them" (Luke 24:30). Jesus taught His followers to ask for daily bread, which implies that we will thank God for our food.

The disciples were familiar with Jesus blessing, breaking, and distributing bread; however, on that night He said something that was new. **Take, eat; this is my body.** Then Jesus **took the cup, and gave thanks, and gave it to them.** He said, **this is my blood.**

These words have been taken in a variety of ways. Herschel H. Hobbs identified four views that have been held historically: "Roman Catholics believe in transubstantiation, or that the elements in the mass actually become the body and blood of Jesus. Lutherans believe in consubstantiation, a modification of the Roman Catholic view. In this view, the body and blood of Jesus are present with the elements. Some other denominations believe in the Lord's Supper as a means of grace. Discounting the above views, they hold that one receives grace by partaking of the Supper. All of these are sacramental in degree. Baptists believe that the elements merely symbolize the body and blood of Jesus, with no saving effect in partaking of them."[1]

Why shouldn't we take Jesus' words as if He were referring to the elements actually becoming His body and His blood? For one thing, Jesus was there in a flesh-and-blood body. He was speaking symbolically, as He so often did. In John's Gospel are several "I am" statements of Jesus. For example, He said, "I am the vine" (John 15:5); but no one claims He was or is a literal vine. "As Jesus holds up a loaf and declares, 'This is my body,' no one listening will ever imagine that he is claiming the bread to be the literal extension of his flesh."[2]

To deny the Lord literally is present in the elements of the Lord's Supper is not enough; we need to affirm where He is present. The Lord's Spirit is present within each believer (Gal. 2:20). He is present wherever two or three meet in His name (Matt. 18:20). Thus whenever we partake of the Lord's Supper we should be aware of Christ's presence in and among us.

The Lord's Supper is a symbol; yet a symbol is important because it stands for the reality. In this case the bread and cup represent His body and blood given on the cross for our sins. **Testament** is the word for "covenant" (NIV, HCSB). Jesus' death on the cross inaugurated the new covenant predicted in Jeremiah 31:31-35. A chief feature of the new covenant is **the remission of sins.** Jesus shed His blood for this purpose. The Lord's Supper was instituted to remind us of that reality.

The wording of verse 27 sounds as if Jesus were telling them to drink the entire cup. However, **all** refers to all of them. With Judas gone, Jesus wanted all of them to understand and to partake.

Verse 29 looks to the future. Jesus told the apostles that He would **not drink henceforth of this fruit of the vine, until that day when** He would **drink it new with** them in His **Father's kingdom.** This is one of several references to heaven including a feast (Matt. 22:1-14; Rev. 19:9). After His resurrection, Jesus ate with His disciples; however, this prophecy looks to the final coming of God's kingdom.

What are the lasting lessons in Matthew 26:26-29?

1. Jesus instituted the Lord's Supper.

2. Jesus' followers should obey Him and partake of the Lord's Supper.

3. Jesus is not literally present in the elements, but He is present in and among His people.

Reminder to the Church (1 Cor. 11:23-26)

Why did Paul mention the Lord's Supper at this point in his letter? What is the evidence that the Lord's Supper originally was taken as part of a meal? What was Paul's source for this description of the Lord's Supper? In what ways are we to remember the Lord? How does the Supper depict past, present, and future aspects of Christ's work? How often should we take the Lord's Supper?

1 Corinthians 11:23-26: **For I have received of the Lord that which also I delivered unto you, That the Lord Jesus the same night in which he was betrayed took bread: [24]and when he had given thanks, he brake it, and said, Take, eat: this is my body, which is broken for you: this do in remembrance of me. [25]After the same manner also he took the cup, when he had supped, saying, This cup is the new testament in my blood: this do ye, as oft as ye drink it, in remembrance of me. [26]For as often as ye eat this bread, and drink this cup, ye do show the Lord's death till he come.**

Jesus instituted the Lord's Supper as part of a Passover meal, and the early church for a while took it with a meal. The Book of Acts often speaks of the early believers breaking bread together. It is hard to know in each such situation whether the language refers to eating together, taking the Lord's Supper, or both. Acts 20:7 says of the believers at Troas, "On the first day of the week we came together to break bread" (NIV). Verse 11 says of Eutychus [YOO-tih-kuhs], who had fallen from a window, that after Paul had restored his life, "He went upstairs again and broke bread and ate" (NIV). John B. Polhill identified the reference in verse 7 as the Lord's Supper. "That the Lord's Supper was accompanied by a larger fellowship meal may be indicated by the reference to their 'eating' in verse 11 (cf. 1 Cor. 11:20f)."[3]

At Corinth, both a meal and the Lord's Supper were eaten together. First Corinthians 11:17-22 refers to some abuses that took place concerning a meal that was supposed to express love for the Lord and for one another. Early in this letter Paul rebuked the Corinthians for dissension concerning preferences for leaders (1:10-13). In 11:17-22 Paul rebuked them for dissension at the fellowship meal. The exact situation is uncertain, but the problem was based on social and economic differences. One purpose of these meals was to feed the poorer members; another purpose was to express fellowship. The richer members arrived earlier and ate the best food before the other group arrived. Paul's words were a rebuke against turning a fellowship meal into an expression of selfishness and dissension. Then Paul presented his teaching concerning the Lord's Supper.

Received and **delivered** became technical words for hearing and telling the teachings and actions of Jesus—**I have received of the Lord that which also I delivered unto you.** The same two words occur in 1 Corinthians 15:3, where Paul wrote of the death, burial, and resurrection as the gospel. In Galatians 1:10–2:10, Paul insisted that he learned his gospel from the Lord, not from the other apostles. Some Bible students believe he also learned about the Lord's Supper by direct revelation. After all, he wrote that he had received it from the Lord. Other Bible students believe that the words **received** and **delivered** show that Paul received the facts about Jesus' coming, life, death, and resurrection from the testimony of eyewitnesses. Both views may have been true. Paul had been told how Jesus instituted the Lord's Supper, but the Lord gave him special insight into its meaning. The Corinthians probably were familiar with how Jesus instituted the Lord's Supper, but Paul wanted them to see how it applied to them.

Much of what is in Matthew 26:23-26 is in 1 Corinthians 11:23-26. Paul, however, included some words of Jesus that are not in Matthew's account (although the words are in Luke 22:17-20). **This do in remembrance of me.** When Christians partake of the Lord's Supper, we remember Christ and His sacrificial death for us. His shed **blood** made possible **the new testament** ("covenant," NIV, HCSB). The Corinthians were familiar with memorial meals designed to keep alive the memory of some prominent person. However, the Lord's Supper is not a memorial meal for a dead person. Christians do not remember a dead Savior. We remember what Christ did when He died for us, but His Spirit is with us. He is not dead but living.

Is the Lord's Supper not also an opportunity to remember our past experiences with the Lord Jesus, especially when He first forgave our sins? John Newton, who wrote the words to "Amazing Grace," felt he needed to remember how God had delivered him from terrible sins. On his mantelpiece was a biblical text: "Thou shalt remember that thou wast a bondman in the land of Egypt, and the Lord thy God redeemed thee." An old Puritan, Thomas Goodwin, wrote his son: "When I was threatening to become cold in my ministry, and when I felt Sabbath morning coming and my heart not filled with amazement at the grace of God, or when I was making ready to dispense the Lord's Supper, do you know what I used to do? I used to take a turn up and down among the sins of my past life, and I always came down again with a broken and contrite heart, ready to preach, as it was preached in the beginning, the forgiveness of sins."[4]

The words, **This do ye, as oft as ye drink it, in remembrance of me** cause us to raise the question, When should we take the Lord's Supper? The Bible does not spell this out. We are baptized once, but we take the Lord's Supper many times. When we do take it, we should do it **in remembrance** of Christ. Also, whenever we take the Lord's Supper, we **show** ("proclaim," NIV, HCSB) **the Lord's death till he come.** Both baptism and the Lord's Supper are the gospel for the eye. That is, each presents in symbolic form pictures of the central realities of the gospel. Another thing they have in common is that they both have aspects that are past, present, and future. The Lord's Supper looks back to the death of Christ and to our experience of forgiveness of sins. The Lord's Supper acknowledges the presence of the Lord within and among us. The Lord's Supper looks ahead to the coming again of the Lord and to the feast of joy with Him.

What are the lasting lessons of 1 Corinthians 11:23-26?

1. Whenever we take the Lord's Supper, we do so in remembrance of Christ.

2. Whenever we take the Lord's Supper, we also remember how Jesus saved us.

3. Whenever we take the Lord's Supper, we look ahead to Jesus' future coming.

Opportunity for Examination (1 Cor. 11:27-32)

*In what ways can people take the Lord's Supper **unworthily**? What did Paul mean by **not discerning the Lord's body**? In what ways should Christians **examine** themselves? How had God disciplined the Corinthians?*

1 Corinthians 11:27-32: Wherefore whosoever shall eat this bread, and drink this cup of the Lord unworthily, shall be guilty of the body and blood of the Lord. [28]But let a man examine himself, and so let him eat of that bread, and drink of that cup. [29]For he that eateth and drinketh unworthily, eateth and drinketh damnation to himself, not discerning the Lord's body. [30]For this cause many are weak and sickly among you, and many sleep. [31]For if we would judge ourselves, we should not be judged. [32]But when we are judged, we are chastened of the Lord, that we should not be condemned with the world.

These verses deal with three basic topics: taking the Lord's Supper in the wrong way, the seriousness of this sin, and how we should take the Lord's Supper. As noted in the Word Study, **unworthily** does not exclude unworthy people from partaking. If unworthy people were not to partake, no one would partake. None of us is worthy. Paul was warning against partaking of the Lord's Supper in an unworthy way. Paul may have had in mind more than one unworthy way, but surely one of the ways was the way the Corinthians took it.

The seriousness of their actions is seen in Paul's charge that their actions made them **guilty of the body and blood of the Lord.** The apostle did not spell out what these words mean, but sinning against the body and blood of Christ is something no believer wants to do. In verse 29 Paul said that they were **not discerning** ("recognizing," NIV, HCSB) **the Lord's body.** What did Paul mean by **body** in the verse? There are two schools of thought on this point. One view is that the word in verse 29 refers to the physical body of Christ who shed His blood to save us. In other words, **body** in verse 29 refers to **the body and blood of the Lord** in verse 27. The other view interprets **body** as the church as the body of Christ. Chapter 12 deals with spiritual gifts within the body of Christ. Another support for this view is the context of 11:17-22, which deals with the church. Each view has its advocates. Whatever Paul meant, both views present ways of taking the Lord's Supper in unworthy ways. Taking this ordinance without reverently remembering the Lord and His death for us would miss the whole point. At the same time, taking the Lord's Supper in a spirit of dissension among members would also be serious. We have seen examples of both actions. A church was taking the Lord's Supper and some boys on the back row were acting as if they were drunk. Such irreverence is surely an unworthy way to take the Lord's Supper. Or you may have been in a church where members who were out of fellowship with one another. How could they truly take the Lord's Supper without first being reconciled to one another? Paul's words can also be taken seriously by anyone who goes through the motions of taking the Lord's Supper without remembering the Lord's death for us.

Paul said that the proper way to take the Lord's Supper is to **examine** yourself. *Dokimazo* is used of the testing of metals. Before and during the Lord's Supper, each believer can conduct a rigorous self-examination. With the help of the Holy Spirit, Christians can place their lives under a spiritual microscope. Many Christians are not comfortable with times for silent meditation and introspection. The Lord's Supper provides a time to be still in the presence of the Lord. Christians who examine themselves open their lives to the true meaning of the Lord's Supper. We can examine our hearts for unconfessed sins, and we can confess our sins and be forgiven. We can examine how close we are to the Lord, and we can draw closer. We can examine our relations with other believers and take steps to seek reconciliation if it is needed.

Those who take the Lord's Supper in unworthy ways face the discipline of divine judgment. Verses 29-32 contain several Greek words containing the word *krino*, which means "judge." **Discerning** (v. 29) is *diakrino*. **Judged** (v. 31) is *krino*. **Condemned** (v. 32) is *katakrino*. Paul also used *krima*, which is translated **damnation** (v. 29), but which probably refers to temporal judgment rather than condemnation to hell. Paul was describing the judgments that came on the Corinthians for taking the Lord's Supper in unworthy ways. Thus he added, **For this cause many are weak and sickly among you, and many sleep.** In other words, Paul attributed some sickness—and even some deaths—to their sins in connection with the Lord's Supper. Paul wrote that they were being **judged** in these ways (v. 32). However, he distinguished these judgments from being **condemned with the world.** He used the word **chastened** ("disciplined," NIV, HCSB) to describe the judgments of illness and death on the Corinthian believers.

What did Paul propose? **If we would judge ourselves, we should not be judged.** "If we were properly evaluating ourselves, we would not be judged" (HCSB). **Judge** translates *diakrino*, the same word translated **discerning** in verse 29. *Diakrino* in verse 29 means "distinguishing between what we are and what we ought to be."[5] Paul's point was that those who examine or evaluate themselves and make appropriate changes avoid severe discipline from God.

Paul was not teaching that all sickness and death among believers is discipline by God because of our sins, but some of it is. Abuses of the Lord's Supper are serious enough to call forth such disciplining judgments from the Lord. This is all the more reason for examining ourselves in connection with taking the Lord's Supper.

What are the lasting lessons in 1 Corinthians 11:27-32?

1. Christians must not take the Lord's Supper in unworthy ways.

2. One unworthy way is to fail to recognize the presence of the crucified Lord.

3. Another unworthy way is to cause dissension by acting selfishly.

4. Christians should examine themselves in connection with the Lord's Supper.

5. Those who fail to do so face God's hand of discipline.

❖ *Spiritual Transformations*

Jesus instituted the Lord's Supper during the last supper with His disciples. He pointed to the elements as symbols of His blood shed for the forgiveness of sins, of His presence in and among believers, and of the gospel being preached until He comes again. After warning of selfish actions of some Corinthians during a fellowship meal prior to the Lord's Supper, Paul reminded them of Jesus' command to take the Lord's Supper in remembrance of Him. He warned of the seriousness of abuses of the Lord's Supper and called the believers to avoid severe discipline from God.

Earlier we noted that the Lord's Supper is a symbol of deep spiritual realities. A symbol is not the reality, but it stands for the reality. As an example, our flag is a symbol of our nation. I believe that we can learn some things about the Lord's Supper by comparing this religious symbol to a national symbol. Americans say a pledge of allegiance to our flag and to our country. We stand and honor our country when the national anthem is sung and the flag flown. What do you think and feel at such times? At times you may only go through the motions, but at other times you feel grateful for our country and renew your commitment to it and your hope for it. At such times you respond personally to the symbol of our land in a way similar to how we honor our Lord by taking the Lord's Supper. Our enemies sometimes tear down our flag, trample on it or burn it. Occasionally Americans do things that dishonor the flag and the land it stands for. Such actions are comparable to taking the Lord's Supper in unworthy ways. Thus just as we ought to honor our country by saluting the flag, even more so should we honor the Lord by taking the Lord's Supper in worthy ways.

In what worthy ways can you partake of the Lord's Supper? _____

Prayer of Commitment: Lord, help me take Your Supper in worthy ways. Amen.

[1]Herschel H. Hobbs, *The Baptist Faith and Message,* rev. ed. [Nashville: Convention Press, 1996], 76).

[2]Craig L. Blomberg, "Matthew," in *The New American Commentary,* vol. 22 [Nashville: Broadman Press, 1992], 390.

[3]Polhill, "Acts," NAC, 418.

[4]F. W. Boreham, *A Bunch of Everlastings* [New York: The Abingdon Press, 1920], 222-223.

[5]Leon Morris, *The First Epistle of Paul to the Corinthians,* rev. ed., in the Tyndale New Testament Commentaries [Grand Rapids: William B. Eerdmans Publishing Company, 1987], 162.

CHURCH LEADERSHIP

Background Passages: 1 Timothy 3:1-7; 5:17-18;
Hebrews 13:7-9,17-18
Focal Passages: 1 Timothy 3:1-7; 5:17-18; Hebrews 13:7,17-18
Key Verse: Hebrews 13:17

❖ *Significance of the Lesson*

• The *Theme* of this lesson is that the church of Jesus Christ needs godly leaders who meet biblical qualifications, and believers have a responsibility to respect and support those leaders.
• The *Life Question* this lesson addresses is, Who can be church leaders and what is my responsibility toward these leaders?
• The *Biblical Truth* is that the church needs biblically qualified people in places of leadership. Leaders and non-leaders have mutual responsibilities to each other.
• The *Life Impact* is to help you support and submit to godly church leaders.

Attitudes Toward Leaders

During the last few decades many people have developed a bias against institutions and their leaders. The church and its leaders have been included in this bias. A natural human resistance to authority reinforces this bias. One result is a lack of respect for leaders of any institution—including the church. The biblical view of the church is that it is Christ's body with many members and that Christ gives to the church gifted leaders who equip the members for their part in the church's ministry. As church leaders seek to fulfill this calling, they deserve the respect of those who hear them preach and teach God's Word. Because of the importance of church leaders, the church should be careful to seek biblically qualified people who have a shepherd's heart.

Word Study: *Bishop*

In Greek culture *episkopos* was used of the presiding officer in a civic or religious organization. In 1 Timothy 3:1 the word can be translated "overseer" (NIV, HCSB). In some denominations, a bishop has the oversight of more than one church. In the New Testament a bishop served in one church. Many people believe that the same church leader is referred to as overseer, pastor, and elder.

❖ *Search the Scriptures*

Paul listed the basic qualifications for church leaders. He taught that a leader is worthy of financial support. The writer to the Hebrews called the people to remember past leaders and to seek to be like them. He challenged the people to obey leaders whom God had made accountable for the people.

Qualifications for Leaders (1 Tim. 3:1-7)

Why did Paul emphasize what a church leader is instead of what he does? What positive qualities did Paul list? What negatives did Paul mention? Why is a leader's home life so important? According to verses 6-7, what two ways might a church leader fall into the devil's snare?

1 Timothy 3:1-7: This is a true saying, If a man desire the office of a bishop, he desireth a good work. [2]A bishop then must be blameless, the husband of one wife, vigilant, sober, of good behavior, given to hospitality, apt to teach; [3]not given to wine, no striker, not greedy of filthy lucre; but patient, not a brawler, not covetous; [4]one that ruleth well his own house, having his children in subjection with all gravity. [5](For if a man know not how to rule his own house, how shall he take care of the church of God?) [6]Not a novice, lest being lifted up with pride he fall into the condemnation of the devil. [7]Moreover he must have a good report of them which are without; lest he fall into reproach and the snare of the devil.

First Timothy is one of Paul's Pastoral Letters. The letter is addressed to his son in the faith, Timothy, and it contains some personal words. Most of the letter, however, deals with how to help churches and their leaders. Thus 1 Timothy 3:1-7 lists the qualifications for **the office of a bishop,** which can also be called "pastor" or "elder."

Only one item in the list describes something a pastor does. Everything else pertains to the kind of person he should be. The work of a church leader is important, but his character is the foundation for what he does.

This is a true ("trustworthy," NIV, HCSB) **saying.** This formula is found five times in Paul's Pastoral Letters. Paul used it to highlight certain statements. Of course, all Paul's sayings were trustworthy, but he drew attention to some.

Paul wrote that being **a bishop** is **a good work** ("noble task," NIV; "noble work," HCSB). In many ways this is God's highest calling. The word translated **desire** ("aspires," HCSB; "sets his heart on being," NIV) is *orego.* It means "to stretch oneself out" or "to aspire to." The word **desireth** translates *epithumeo.* This word can refer to a selfish desire, but it also can refer to a desire motivated by love and commitment. We don't usually think of this vocation as one that a person seeks. Paul was not denying that God's calling should precede a desire to be a pastor, but he was teaching that those who respond positively to this high calling show wisdom and discernment.

George W. Truett told a group of fellow preachers: "Now, for a generation, I have given my humble testimony, as a preacher of his glorious gospel. If he should give me a thousand lives, today, and ask me to choose what calling I would have them follow, I would not hesitate one moment, to choose that every one of the thousand lives should be a preacher for him."[1]

The first qualification is that the person be **blameless** ("above reproach," NIV, HCSB). The person should have no skeletons in his closet, no past or present sins that will cut the ground out from under any pastor. This applies to the consistency of the man's life since his conversion. Some church leaders did evil things before coming to Christ. Paul himself would have been disqualified from being a church leader if his former life were held against him. But after he became a believer, he lived a life dedicated to Christ.

The requirement to be **the husband of one wife** has been subject to a number of interpretations. Thomas D. Lea mentioned five. (1) The pastor must be married. (2) The pastor cannot remarry after his wife dies. (3) The pastor cannot practice polygamy. (4) The pastor cannot have been divorced. (5) The pastor must be faithful to his wife. Lea discounted the first two because of Paul's preference for remaining single (1 Cor. 7:32-35) and because Paul allowed widowed Christians to remarry if they married believers (v. 39). Paul and the early believers opposed polygamy

based on the biblical view of marriage (Gen. 2:24). The last two interpretations are the most likely to contain Paul's meaning. Lea gave
special emphasis to the fifth one. "The Greek describes the overseer literally as a 'one-woman kind of man' (cf. 'faithful to his one wife,' NEB)."[2]
Many Baptists, however, believe that Paul was referring to divorce.

The next three qualities are closely related. **Vigilant** ("self-
controlled," HCSB; "temperate," NIV) describes a mental self-control
that does not act rashly and impulsively. **Sober** ("sensible," HCSB)
refers to a person who is balanced in judgment. A person **of good behavior** is "respectable" (NIV, HCSB) not by reason of birth but because
his actions gain the respect of others inside and outside the church.

Being **given to hospitality** was important in an age without many safe
places for travelers. Christian missionaries such as Paul traveled a lot.
So did rank-and-file believers such as Aquila and Priscilla. A number of
New Testament passages stress hospitality (1 Tim. 5:10; Heb. 13:2;
3 John 6-8). A church leader must be willing to welcome believing travelers.

He must be **apt to teach** ("an able teacher," HCSB; "able to teach,"
NIV). Ephesians 4:11 lists "pastors and teachers" among the gifted
people whom the Lord gives as gifts to the church. Although some
leaders were mostly teachers, this passage probably refers to pastors
who teach. Paul surely listed teaching ability among the qualifications
for pastors. In fact, teaching is the only task in verses 1-7.

Verse 3 is a list of mostly negative qualities a pastor must not have.
The inclusion of these shows the kind of sinful conduct that charac-
terized much first-century life. Many pastors probably were from an
old life in which these things were done. **Not given to wine** ("drunkenness," NIV) means that he must not be "addicted to wine" (HCSB).
"In our American society satiated with a thirst for alcohol, the practice
of total abstinence by Christians could curb the destructive effects
alcoholism has brought to us."[3] Two biblical principles provide reasons
for abstinence. One principle is the stewardship of one's health (1 Cor.
6:19-20). The other principle is influence (Rom. 14:20-21). A pastor
who drinks can influence others to do the same.

Violence is closely related to drunkenness. The word **striker** refers to
hitting someone. A pastor must not be "violent, but gentle" (NIV). A violent person is often "a bully" (HCSB) who uses his fists to get his way or
to make his point. He ought to be a gentle person like Jesus. **A brawler** is
a "quarrelsome" (NIV, HCSB) person who relies on verbal abuse to get his
way. Both physical abuse and verbal abuse are totally wrong for a pastor.

A good pastor is **not covetous** ("greedy," HCSB). Literally he is "not a lover of money" (NIV). Paul later warned against thinking of godliness as a means of great gain (1 Tim. 6:5). He was speaking of religious leaders who saw in religion a means of financial gain for themselves. He warned that "the love of money is a root of all kinds of evil" (6:10, HCSB).

Verses 4-5 focus on the pastor's family life. Paul already had mentioned marriage; now he enlarged the subject to include the entire family. Four expressions call for some comment: **ruleth . . . subjection . . . gravity . . . take care of.** Comparing other translations may help. "One who manages his own household competently, having his children under control with all dignity. (If anyone does know how to manage his own household, how will he take care of God's church?)" (HCSB). "He must manage his own family well and see that his children obey him with proper respect. (If anyone does not know how to manage his own family, how can he take care of God's church?)" (NIV).

Rule translates *proistemi,* which literally means "to stand before" and came to mean "manage," "be at the head of," or "rule." The harsh sound of this word, which appears in verses 4 and 5, is softened by its use with **take care of.** This word is *epimeleomai,* which appears in the parable of the good Samaritan to describe how the Samaritan took care of the wounded man and what the Samaritan told the innkeeper to do (Luke 10:34-35). Commenting on the word **rule,** Thomas Lea wrote: "The term demands an effective exercise of authority bolstered by a character of integrity and sensitive compassion. Its use in verse 5 with the verb 'take care of' defines the quality of leadership as related more to showing mercy than to delivering ultimatums."[4]

Verse 6 deals with the danger of **pride.** One way to try to avoid pride is not to have **a novice** ("new convert," HCSB; recent convert," NIV) serve as a pastor. The new convert may well become a pastor after he has had time to mature in the faith, but a new convert is vulnerable to be **lifted up with pride** and thus **fall into the condemnation of the devil.** Since pride was the devil's initial sin, he seeks to lead others to share the judgment of God on pride. A new convert is especially vulnerable. However, pride is not the exclusive domain of new converts. All Christians continue to struggle to overcome the powerful yet subtle temptation to pride. This includes men who have years of experience as pastors. Being in a position of respect and influence can tempt a person to take credit for what only the Lord can do.

Verse 7 ends the list by coming back to the importance of being without reproach in the eyes of outsiders: **He must have a good report of them which are without** ("a good reputation among outsiders," HCSB). This is needed **lest he fall into reproach** ("disgrace," HCSB) **and the snare of the devil.** This does not mean that he seeks popularity at the expense of standing up for and speaking out in ways that may offend some outsiders. It means that outsiders know that he is a person who is true to his calling and convictions. Nothing hurts a church so much as leaders who live like the world rather than representing Christ. Sin in the life of any believer sets a stumbling block in front of outsiders; but because of his wider influence, sin in a pastor's life does the greatest harm to the cause of Christ.

What are the lasting lessons in 1 Timothy 3:1-7?

1. Church leaders should meet biblical qualifications.
2. A pastor's life should be above reproach.
3. He should have basic character traits that are positive.
4. He should not commit the sins of the world.
5. His family life should be exemplary.
6. He must beware of the sin of pride.

Support for Leaders (1 Tim. 5:17-18)

*In what sense do elders **rule**? Were the elders who taught and preached a separate group from those who ruled? In what way did they deserve **double honor**? What authority did Paul claim for paying elders? What was Paul's personal practice about expecting financial support?*

1 Timothy 5:17-18: Let the elders that rule well be counted worthy of double honor, especially they who labor in the word and doctrine. ¹⁸For the scripture saith, Thou shalt not muzzle the ox that treadeth out the corn. And, The laborer is worthy of his reward.

The Greek word *presbyteros* means an older man. Paul used it that way in 1 Timothy 5:1. The word was also used to describe church leaders (v. 17). Baptists generally identify **elders** as referring to the same office as bishops and pastors. **Rule** is the same word used in 3:4-5. In those verses it was used parallel with the word for taking care of one's family. Paul could have used stronger words if he had intended to say that elders were to rule like kings or masters. In 1 Peter 5:1-4 the Apostle Peter wrote to fellow elders and clearly forbade them against "lording it over those entrusted to you" (NIV, HCSB). "Lording it over" translates a word meaning to act as a master does toward a slave *(katakurieuo)*. Instead, Peter said that they should act as shepherds of their flock. This included exercising oversight.

Some Bible students think that verse 17 refers to two separate groups of elders: ruling elders and elders who taught and preached. Others believe that elders had administrative duties and duties related to **the word.** The wording of the verse does not rule out either view. One's view of this depends on one's understanding of church officers and organization. The *Holman Christian Standard Bible* assumes that all elders have some administrative duties and some of these also preach and teach: "The elders who are good leaders should be considered worthy of an ample honorarium, especially those who work hard at preaching and teaching."

This translation interprets **double honor** as "an ample honorarium." Others understand these words to include more than financial support. "The term 'honor' does not refer merely to an honorarium, but the failure to give proper pay would imply a lack of honor. The idea of 'double' may refer to the double portion the oldest in the family received (Deut. 21:17). It probably consisted of the twin benefits of honor or respect and financial remuneration."[5]

Paul supported his call for financial support for pastors by quoting Deuteronomy 25:4: **Thou shalt not muzzle the ox that treadeth out the corn.** The Israelites were supposed to allow the ox to eat some of the grain his work produced. Paul also quoted words of Jesus found in Luke 10:7: **The laborer is worthy of his reward.** Thus Paul used **scripture** to support his position. Paul dealt with this sensitive subject in 1 Corinthians 9:1-23. He established his right to expect pay for his ministry, but he had voluntarily given up this right in Corinth. He felt the inner compulsion to preach the gospel, but he gave up the right to accept pay when doing so would help advance the cause of Christ. Paul said that he could choose not to accept pay, but he could not choose not to preach the gospel.

What are the lasting lessons of 1 Timothy 5:17-18?

1. Leaders who preach and teach God's Word deserve respect and remuneration.

2. The need to pay pastors is based on Scripture.

Follow Leaders' Examples (Heb. 13:7)

*How does verse 7 fit into the context of Hebrews? What evidence is there that the words apply to dead leaders? Why did Paul ask readers to **remember** these leaders?*

Hebrews 13:7: Remember them which have the rule over you, who have spoken unto you the word of God: whose faith follow, considering the end of their conversation.

The Book of Hebrews is a book of exhortations interspersed among doctrinal sections. The doctrinal sections presents Jesus and the new covenant as superior to the old covenant. The exhortations include words of challenge, warning, and encouragement. The readers had successfully endured some persecution but no one had been killed (10:32-39; 12:4). Worse persecution was coming, and they needed to have faith and demonstrate faithfulness.

The final chapter is a series of short exhortations on a variety of subjects. Three have to do with leaders (vv. 7,17,24). The writer seemed to have begun with a call to **remember** dead leaders. Hebrews 11 challenges readers to remember the heroes of faith from Old Testament times. Now 13:7 challenges readers to remember church leaders who had **spoken unto** them **the word of God.** Hebrews 2:3 shows that the readers of Hebrews were second-generation believers. The earliest leaders spoke as eyewitnesses. The writer seemed to consider himself and other current leaders as those who built on the early preaching. Perhaps it was during the lifetimes of these early leaders that the people proved faithful in persecution: "But call to remembrance the former days, in which, after ye were illumined, ye endured a great fight of afflictions" (10:32).

The meaning of two words in 13:7 needs to be clarified. **End** is *ekbasis,* which here refers to the end or "outcome" (NIV, HCSB) of their lives. **Conversation** is *anastrophe,* which refers to a way of life. "As you carefully observe the outcome of their lives, imitate their faith" (HCSB).

Most believers have memories of a former pastor or someone else who has gone to be with the Lord. They provide examples for us to follow. I have such memories of the pastor of my childhood, youth, and young adult years. Especially in my early years as a pastor, I followed his example in many ways. Who provided for you a good example that you have tried to follow?

Verse 7 is closely related to verse 8. Earthly leaders come and go, but "Jesus Christ" is "the same yesterday, and today, and forever."

What are the lasting lessons in Hebrews 13:7?

1. Remember past church leaders whose faith and life were good examples.

2. Follow their examples.

3. We do not have to wait until spiritual leaders are deceased to follow their faithful examples.

Submit to and Pray for Leaders (Heb. 13:17-18)

What word for **rule** *is used? In what ways are members to* **obey** *leaders? How does verse 17 fit into the context of Hebrews? Why did the author of Hebrews ask them to* **pray for us**?

Hebrews 13:17-18: Obey them that have the rule over you, and submit yourselves: for they watch for your souls, as they that must give account, that they may do it with joy, and not with grief: for that is unprofitable for you. [18]Pray for us: for we trust we have a good conscience, in all things willing to live honestly.

The word for **rule** in Hebrews 13:7,17,24 is different from the word in 1 Timothy 3:4-5 and 5:17. The word in Hebrews is *hegeomai.* Luke used this word in Luke 22:26 to describe Jesus' words as He rebuked the apostles for their selfish desire to be greatest. Jesus defined the best leaders as servants. Obeying and submitting to servant-leaders is what verse 17 calls for. Such leaders accept accountability for the **souls** of those whom they lead and serve. "Obey your leaders and submit to them, for they keep watch over your souls as those who will give an account, so that they can do this with joy and not with grief, for that would be unprofitable for you" (HCSB).

People's view of church government determines how they interpret and apply the words **obey** and **submit.** People in some forms of church government are expected to obey the person or group that run the church. Baptists have a congregational form of government in which each member stands on equal ground. Christ Himself is the head of the church, and God's Word is the authority to which believers submit. A pastor's authority grows out of his teaching and preaching God's Word and his faithfulness in following Christ and calling others to follow Him.

The author of Hebrews may have been a church leader who was away for a time. He was certainly a supporter of the church's leaders. He found out that some church members were not following the Lord as they should. The church leaders were calling them to follow Christ all the way. The author agreed with this emphasis and wrote to call the members to obey their leaders.

As one of their leaders, the author asked his readers to **pray for** him and the other church leaders. His use of the plural **we** is the reason for interpreting his prayer request to include all their present leaders. Church members should pray for their pastor and other church leaders. Charles H. Spurgeon was one of the most effective preachers of the 19th century. His proclamation of Christ from God's Word drew people to a 6,000 seat tabernacle. Someone asked Spurgeon the secret of his power in preaching. Without hesitating, Spurgeon said, "My people pray for me."[6]

What are the lasting lessons in Hebrews 13:17-18?

1. Pastors use God's Word to call people to follow Christ.
2. Members should obey their leaders as they fulfill this task.
3. Members should pray for church leaders.

❖ Spiritual Transformations

Paul listed the qualifications for a bishop (elder, pastor). He said that elders who preach and teach the Word ought to receive a double honor, which includes financial support. The author of Hebrews called his readers to remember past leaders and to imitate their faith and way of living. He called readers to obey and submit to leaders who used God's Word to call people to follow Christ.

In your opinion, what do church leaders owe church members? __

_____

What do church members owe church leaders?

_____

Prayer of Commitment: Lord, be with those who serve as pastors and help them fulfill their calling. Help me fulfill my responsibilities to You as head of the church and to leaders whom you have called to teach and preach God's Word. Amen.

[1]George W. Truett, *"Follow Thou Me"* [Nashville: Broadman Press, n. d.], 230.
[2]Thomas D. Lea, "1,2 Timothy, Titus," in *The New American Commentary*, vol. 34 [Nashville: Broadman Press, 1992], 109-110.
[3]Lea, "1,2 Timothy, Titus," NAC, 111.
[4]Lea, "1,2 Timothy, Titus," NAC, 112.
[5]Lea, "1,2 Timothy," NAC, 155.
[6]Theodore F. Adams, *Tell Me How* [New York: Harper & Row, Publishers, 1964], 105.

SPIRITUAL GIFTS

Background Passage: 1 Corinthians 12:1-30
Focal Passage: 1 Corinthians 12:4-15,20,27
Key Verses: 1 Corinthians 12:12-14

❖ *Significance of the Lesson*

• The *Theme* of this lesson is that the Holy Spirit empowers all believers with spiritual gifts that they should use to glorify God and edify His people.
• The *Life Question* this lesson addresses is, What is the purpose of spiritual gifts and how can I use mine in a way that pleases God?
• The *Biblical Truth* is that spiritual gifts are to build up the body of Christ, the church, not to build up the individual exercising the gift.
• The *Life Impact* is to help you discover and exercise your spiritual gifts.

Attitudes About Spiritual Gifts

Many Christians do not know they have spiritual gifts, while others are not concerned about using their gifts in the church. On the other hand, some Christians overemphasize certain spiritual gifts. Paul exhorted members of the Corinthian church to exercise their gifts in a way to build up the body of Christ and to realize that all gifts are interdependent just as are the parts of a human body.

Now Concerning Spiritual Gifts

The Corinthians had sent Paul a letter that asked about several issues (7:1). Paul introduced each subject with the words "now concerning" (7:1; 8:1; 12:1). In the first two of these Paul quoted something from their letter, but he did not quote what they said or asked in 12:1. We can only guess what they wrote by reading how Paul responded in chapters 12–14. Chapter 12 presents the diversity of spiritual gifts and emphasizes that all are gifts of God to be used for the good of the church. Chapter 13 shows that no gift is as important as the spirit of love with which the gift is used. Chapter 14 presents reasons why Paul preferred gifts that build up the church in contrast to gifts that benefit only the individual.

❖ *Search the Scriptures*

Paul presented the Triune God as the source of spiritual gifts and the common good as their purpose. He named some of the diverse gifts. Using the analogy of the parts of the human body, Paul stressed the unifying purpose of God for each and all the spiritual gifts.

Purpose of Gifts (1 Cor. 12:4-7)

In what sense is each Christian "gifted"? What is the source of spiritual gifts? What is the purpose of spiritual gifts?

Verses 4-7: Now there are diversities of gifts, but the same Spirit. [5]And there are differences of administrations, but the same Lord. [6]And there are diversities of operations, but it is the same God which worketh all in all. [7]But the manifestation of the Spirit is given to every man to profit withal.

Paul used two different words to describe spiritual **gifts** in 1 Corinthians 12. He used *pneumatikon* in verse 1. He used *charismaton* in verse 4 and throughout the chapter (vv. 9,28,30,31; see also Rom. 12:6). The first word is related to the word *Spirit, pneuma.* The latter word is from the same root as *charis* or *grace* and means a gift that has been freely and generously given. The first word emphasizes the Spirit as the source of spiritual gifts; the other stresses that they are gifts.

Often we use *gifted* to describe a person with natural talents or abilities. Whatever talent or aptitude we possess is a gift from God. This is certainly true of spiritual gifts. A spiritual gift is a gift and trust from God. Rather than taking credit for such gifts, we should give thanks to God.

All spiritual gifts have one source. They all come from **the same Spirit.** Notice the parallels in verses 4-6. **Gifts** in verse 4 is parallel to **administrations** in verse 5 and **operations** in verse 6. **Spirit** in verse 4 is parallel to **Lord** in verse 5 and **God** in verse 6. In essence Paul emphasized His main point by saying it three different ways.

Administrations translates *diakonion,* a familiar word meaning "ministries" (HCSB) or "services" (NRSV). The different spiritual gifts make possible the many and varied ministries of the church. Paul connected these church ministries with **the same Lord.**

Operations translates *energematon,* a word meaning "activities" (HCSB) or "effects" (NASB). Gordon D. Fee wrote, "The emphasis seems to be on the 'effects' produced by work, not simply on activity in and of itself."[1] Our word *energy* comes from the root of this word. The power for the ministries of spiritual gifts comes from **the same God.** Every effect of the exercise of spiritual gifts is not a human accomplishment, but a work of God. "The same God is active in everyone and everything" (HCSB).

Verses 4-6 mention **the same Spirit . . . the same Lord . . . the same God.** This is one of many biblical references to the one God as Father, Son, and Spirit (Matt. 3:16-17; 28:19; 2 Cor. 13:14). The doctrine of the Trinity is based on two realities: (1) this is how God has revealed Himself; (2) this is how we have experienced Him. The different kinds of spiritual gifts and ministries come from one source: the one God who gives the gifts, inspires the ministries, and makes possible the desired results.

Verse 7 reemphasizes that each spiritual gift is a **manifestation of the Spirit.** Then Paul added two new thoughts. The first of these is implicit in earlier verses, but here he spelled it out. At least one gift **is given to every man** ("each person," HCSB). No one can claim on biblical grounds that he or she has received no gift of grace from God's Spirit. You may not yet know what the gift is, but according to God's Word, you have at least one.

In the final part of verse 7 Paul focused on the purpose of spiritual gifts. All the gifts are given **to profit withal.** This translates *pros to sympheron,* literally meaning "for the benefit, advantage, or profit." Paul did not at this point spell out for whose benefit. Some translations leave open this issue—"A manifestation of the Spirit is given to each person to produce what is beneficial" (HCSB). Many translations, however, assume that the larger context makes clear that an individual gift is not just for that person's good but also for the good of the church as a whole—"Now to each one the manifestation of the Spirit is given for the common good" (NIV). Later in the chapter Paul wrote that God had given different gifts "that there should be no schism in the body; but that the members should have the same care for one another" (v. 25).

What are the lasting lessons in 1 Corinthians 12:4-7?

1. Christians are gifted people whom God has entrusted with spiritual gifts.

2. God gives at least one gift to each member of the body of Christ.

3. God wants us to use the gifts He gives for the good of the church, not just to benefit ourselves.

Diversity of Gifts (1 Cor. 12:8-10)

What gifts are listed in these verses? How do these gifts compare to Paul's other lists of spiritual gifts? Are these biblical lists representative of gifts, or are these biblical lists the only spiritual gifts? How can believers discover their own gifts?

Verses 8-10: For to one is given by the Spirit the word of wisdom; to another the word of knowledge by the same Spirit; [9]to another faith by the same Spirit; to another the gifts of healing by the same Spirit; [10]to another the working of miracles; to another prophecy; to another discerning of spirits; to another divers kinds of tongues; to another the interpretation of tongues.

Paul listed nine gifts in verses 8-10. The first two are so closely related that some consider them the same gift. The Corinthians prized both **wisdom** and **knowledge.** Paul challenged their view of wisdom with the wisdom of the cross (1:18-31). He insisted that true wisdom is the opposite of the kind of pride displayed by the bickering members of the Corinthians (2:1–3:3). They took pride in what they considered their superior knowledge; but Paul said that such knowledge puffs up in contrast to love, which builds up (8:1). Wisdom in the Bible often refers to insight into how to live as God intends. Knowledge may refer to special insight into the Scriptures. The gift of teaching is not found in verses 8-10, but it is found in all of Paul's lists of gifts. Thus the kind of wisdom and knowledge Paul had in mind may relate especially to teaching. This view is strengthened by the use of **the word of wisdom** and **the word of knowledge,** implying that these two gifts of the Spirit have to do with words.

The next three gifts have to do with supernatural power. Paul listed **faith** as a spiritual gift. He meant something more than the kind of faith that all believers have (Eph. 2:8-9). Jesus taught that faith as small as a grain of mustard seed can move mountains (Matt. 17:20). Based on what Paul wrote in 1 Corinthians 13:2, this seems to have been what he meant in 12:9. This kind of faith is closely related to the **gifts of healing,** which is one expression of the **working of miracles.**

Prophecy is in all Paul's lists of spiritual gifts. Like the Old Testament prophets, some of their messages were predictions (Acts 11:27-28; 21:10-11); but most prophets declared God's message for their listeners. We know from chapter 14 (see vv. 1-5) that this gift was expressed in language understood by hearers and that it was useful in building up the church. The prophets were valuable leaders in the churches (Eph. 2:20).

Discerning of spirits ("distinguishing between spirits," HCSB, NIV) is the gift of discerning whether a person is led by God's Spirit. Many claimed to be led by the Spirit of God, but not all were led by Him. John wrote, "Dear friends, do not believe every spirit, but test the spirits to determine if they are from God, because many false prophets have gone out into the world" (1 John 4:1, HCSB). There are some tests that every Christian can apply, but some believers are specifically equipped by the Spirit to distinguish true from false spirits.

The final two gifts are mentioned only in 1 Corinthians. Both have to do with the gift of **tongues.** The word *glossa* can mean "tongue," "speaking," or "language." Some translations use **divers kinds of tongues** ("speaking in different kinds of tongues," NIV) to describe what Paul meant. Others have "different kinds of languages" (HCSB). Some Bible students believe that Paul was referring to foreign languages, but others believe the Corinthians were practicing a kind of ecstatic speech that was unintelligible to the hearers. When the crowd at Pentecost heard the witnesses for Jesus, they said, "We hear them speaking in our own languages" (HCSB), or "We hear them . . . in our own tongues!" (Acts 2:11, NIV). Most, therefore, believe that the tongues at Pentecost were actual languages. But the question is, Did Paul mean that the tongues at Corinth were languages—as at Pentecost—or was he referring to unintelligible speech? At any rate, chapter 14 shows that the listeners could not understand the people speaking in tongues.

Paul's letters contain several lists of spiritual gifts. In addition to 1 Corinthians 12:8-10, there also are lists in verses 28-30; Romans 12:6-8; and Ephesians 4:11. Each list has some differences. If each gift were listed on a chart, there would be about 20 gifts. However, some of these may be the same gift using different words.

Three general observations are in order. First, although some people feel that the only valid spiritual gifts are on at least one of the biblical lists, the variety of gifts strongly implies that Paul was not developing a definitive and exhaustive list of possible spiritual gifts. The Spirit may grace someone with a gift that is not spelled out in the Bible.

The second observation is that none of the gifts excuses us from bearing the fruit of the Spirit and fulfilling the basic practices of the Christian faith. In other words, if I have the gift of prophecy, this does not constitute my total responsibility. I can't say that I don't need to show mercy because showing mercy is not one of my gifts.

Third, keep in mind that spiritual gifts were given to be used. Do not neglect your gift, and do not use it for your own advantage. Use it for the glory of God and the needs of others.

What is your spiritual gift? Each believer has at least one. How can a Christian discover his or her gift? You can study the spiritual gifts of the Bible. You can ask God to reveal what your gift is. You can ask other Christians what they think is your gift. Exercise your spiritual gift.

What are the lasting lessons in 1 Corinthians 12:8-10?

1. Paul listed a wide variety of spiritual gifts.

2. Christians are to bear the fruit of the Spirit as they exercise their spiritual gifts.

3. Christians should discover and use their spiritual gifts.

Unity of Gifts (1 Corinthians 12:11-15,20,27)

Who determines what gift each person receives? What biblical analogies describe the church? What realities create the unity of the church? What lessons did Paul teach by word pictures of body parts as church members and their gifts? Why did Paul keep mentioning the one body with many members?

Verses 11-13: **But all these worketh that one and the selfsame Spirit, dividing to every man severally as he will. [12]For as the body is one, and hath many members, and all the members of that one body, being many, are one body: so also is Christ. [13]For by one Spirit are we all baptized into one body, whether we be Jews or Gentiles, whether we be bond or free; and have been all made to drink into one Spirit.**

The wide variety of spiritual gifts is under the sovereign control of God through His Spirit. Notice the repetition of **the same Spirit** in verses 8-9. Paul added to this formula in verse 11 when he wrote of **that one and the selfsame Spirit** ("one and the same Spirit," NIV, HCSB). These words reaffirm that God is the source of the spiritual gifts, that He gives the gifts through His Spirit, and that this one source creates a unity within the church.

Although the Spirit gives gifts to all members of the church, He deals with us one by one individually. This is the meaning of the words **dividing to every man severally** ("distributing to each one," HCSB). This reinforces the point in verse 7 that each person is given at least one gift.

The main emphasis in verse 11 comes in the words **as he will.** That is, "he gives them to each one, just as he determines" (NIV). The *Contemporary English Version* reads, "But it is the Spirit who does all this and decides which gifts to give to each of us." We don't choose what gifts we want; we seek to discover which gifts God has chosen to give us. This is His work, and He apportions individual gifts according to His will and purpose.

For the first time in chapter 12, the word **body** appears in verse 12. The word *church* is not used, but Paul obviously was speaking of the church as a body. The word *church* is used in verse 28 to show clearly that the church is the body of Christ.

The word **for** in verse 12 points back to verses 4-11. In verses 4-6 Paul stressed the oneness of the church. In verses 7-11 he wrote of the variety of spiritual gifts in the church. Verse 12 brings together both the oneness and the diversity. First, Paul focused attention on the body as a whole, recognizing that **the body is one, and hath many members.** That is like seeing the forest and then recognizing it has many trees. Then he looked at the many trees and recognized they are parts of one forest: **The members of that one body, being many, are one body.** When we are emphasizing the unity and oneness, we must remember the many parts. Likewise, when we focus on the diverse parts, we must remember they are parts of one body.

We might expect Paul to end the verse with the words "so also is the church." Instead he wrote **so also is Christ.** These words may be a metonymy, a figure of speech in which one thing is named for that which is closely associated with it. For example, we might speak of *reading Shakespeare* when we really mean *reading the works of Shakespeare.* Thus the last part of verse 12 implies "so also is Christ's church."

Verse 13 emphasizes the oneness of the church but in terms of Christians' experience of the **one Spirit.** Many translations read **by one Spirit. By** translates the Greek preposition *en.* The word then suggests agency; that is, the Spirit does the baptizing—**by one Spirit are we all baptized into one body.** Some translations use "in" to translate *en.* If this is its meaning, the Spirit is the element in which people are baptized—"For in the one Spirit we were all baptized into one body" (NRSV). Either translation suggests that Paul was not focusing on water baptism but on Spirit baptism. The same basic point is made by the words **have been all made to drink into one Spirit** ("we were all given the one Spirit to drink," NIV). Paul was describing our experience with the Spirit in two ways, but his point is the same. We cannot experience the same Spirit without being related to others who also have experienced Him.

This oneness and belonging to the Lord takes precedence over the usual things that separate people. In normal society **Jews** and **Gentiles** ("Greeks," NIV, HCSB) went their separate ways. Each group often harbored negative feelings toward the other group. Yet believers from both groups experienced the same Spirit and thus were spiritually members of a more important group than their ethnic identity. First-century society drew sharp distinctions between slaves and free people; yet in the one Spirit their spiritual oneness made no distinction between **bond** and **free.** The squabbling Corinthians especially needed this call to oneness. Nearly everything became a subject of controversy among them. Their diversity became divisive. They argued about everything from loyalty to leaders to meat sacrificed to idols. Spiritual gifts had become another battlefield for them.

Verses 14-15,20,27: **For the body is not one member, but many. [15]If the foot shall say, Because I am not the hand, I am not of the body; is it therefore not of the body?**

. . . .

[20]But now are they many members, yet but one body.

. . . .

[27]Now ye are the body of Christ, and members in particular.

Having emphasized the unity of the church, Paul again stressed its diversity. He probably had in mind those in the church who thought of themselves as the church but had little room for members who were different from them in some way. In chapters 12–14 they were the ones who considered their spiritual gifts to be superior to others' gifts. Verse 14 states clearly that **the body is not one member, but many.**

Verse 15 introduces a long passage in which Paul used parts of a human body to teach lessons about the exercise of spiritual gifts within the body of Christ. Paul imagined a **foot** saying, **Because I am not the hand, I am not of the body.** In this word picture, the foot may represent members who felt their gifts were not as important as those gifts represented by the hand. Some translations make the last part of verse 15 a question: **Is it therefore not part of the body?** In other words, the foot is part of the body. It may be perceived as less important than the hand, but the foot is an important part of the body. Some translations see the last part of verse 15 as a statement:

"In spite of this it still belongs to the body" (HCSB). The ear is pictured making the same false assumption about the eye (v. 16).

Verse 17 challenges readers to picture what a body would look like if it were one big eye. Perhaps Paul was addressing those members who thought they were superior. His point was stated in verse 14. No one member or gift is the entire body (vv. 18-19). Verse 20 repeats the fact that there are **many members, yet but one body.** No member of the body can say to any other member, "I don't need you!" (v. 21, NIV, HCSB). Even the weaker or unseen parts are needed (vv. 22-25). Each is needed, and all are interdependent: "So if one member suffers, all the members suffer with it; if one member is honored, all the members rejoice with it" (v. 26, HCSB). **Now ye are the body of Christ, and members in particular** ("and individual members of it," HCSB). Each Christian is an individual, but each is also a member of Christ's body.

What are the lasting lessons in 1 Corinthians 12:11-15,20,27?

1. Christians do not choose their spiritual gifts; God apportions them according to His will.

2. The church is the body of Christ.

3. Our common experience of His Spirit makes us one.

4. Each member is important to the body, and all are interdependent.

❖ *Spiritual Transformations*

God entrusts spiritual gifts for the good of the church as a whole. His gifts are different. The Spirit apportions them according to His will. The church is like the human body in that one body consists of many interdependent members.

Do you see your church as a convenience or as a channel for giving and serving? _____

What is your spiritual gift? _____

How are you actively involved in your church by exercising your gift?

_____

Prayer of Commitment: Lord, help me discover and exercise Your gift for Your glory and for the good of the church. Amen.

[1]Gordon D. Fee, *The First Epistle to the Corinthians*, in The New International Commentary on the New Testament [Grand Rapids: William B. Eerdmans Publishing Company, 1987], 587.

Study Theme

That's Encouraging!

When a pastor looks into the faces of the people gathered to worship, he realizes that all kinds of needs are represented. Very likely some of the people are just barely hanging on. In some situations, a word of encouragement can mean the difference between giving up and going on. As I've grown older, I've become increasingly convinced that many people need some word of hope and encouragement. This is also true of those who come to Sunday School.

Fortunately the Word of God is filled with examples and themes that offer just what all of us need. This study theme focuses on four encouraging truths in the Bible: no one is excluded from God's love, believers can have assurance of their salvation, each person can do something useful for God, and people can live with hope and joy even when the worst comes. These are all truths that cause us to say, "That's encouraging!"

The first of the four lessons, "Encouraged by Enduring Love," is based on the assurance of God's faithfulness in Lamentations 3:19-24 and on the story of Christ's loving acceptance of Zacchaeus in Luke 19:1-10. The second lesson, "Encouraged by Sure Salvation," is based on verses from 1 John, which was written so that believers could know they have eternal life (5:13). This is the **Evangelism Lesson** for this quarter. The third lesson, "Encouraged by Redemptive Usefulness," is based on the story of how God led Nehemiah to rally and lead the people of Jerusalem to rebuild their city wall. The fourth lesson, "Encouraged by Faithful Hope," is based on key verses from the Book of Habakkuk, which show how God dealt with questions asked by Habakkuk in leading him to a faith that could rejoice in the Lord even when the worst happened.

This study theme is designed to help you:
- live in the constant assurance of God's love (July 4)
- live with assurance of salvation (July 11)
- live as a useful servant of God (July 18)
- live with hope in God (July 25)

ENCOURAGED BY ENDURING LOVE

Bible Passages: Lamentations 3:19-24; Luke 19:1-10
Key Verse: Lamentations 3:22

❖ *Significance of the Lesson*

• The *Theme* of this lesson is that we can be encouraged in knowing that God loves us, regardless of who we are or what we have done.

• The *Life Question* this lesson addresses is, Why should I believe God loves me?

• The *Biblical Truth* is that God's love endures eternally and includes everyone.

• The *Life Impact* is to help you live in the confident assurance of God's love.

Attitudes Toward God's Love

People struggle with the concept of God's love. When God's existence is acknowledged, He is often perceived as impersonal, cold, distant, demanding, or indifferent. Some cannot reconcile the idea of a loving God with the evil and suffering in the world. Some feel that their lives have been such that God is either unwilling or incapable of loving them. The testimony of Scripture, however, is that God's love continues in spite of circumstances, either internal or external.

Word Study: *Mercies*

Hesed is one of several Old Testament words for love. This word, which appears in Lamentations 3:22, emphasizes God's relation to the people with whom He made a covenant. It focuses on God's loyalty and faithfulness to His people, even when they go astray. Thus it has a note of mercy in it.

❖ *Search the Scriptures*

In the Book of Lamentations, Jeremiah lamented the fall of Jerusalem; however, he praised the faithful love of God for His sinful people. Zacchaeus was disliked because he was a rich tax collector, but Jesus showed God's love for him. As a result, Zacchaeus was changed. The three outline points answer the Life Question.

God's Love Never Ceases (Lam. 3:19-24)

What was the setting for the Book of Lamentations? How do verses 19-20 reflect much of the book's content? What hymn was inspired by verses 21-24? How can we explain these few positive verses in the midst of so much grief and suffering?

Lamentations 3:19-20: Remembering mine affliction and my misery, the wormwood and the gall. ²⁰My soul hath them still in remembrance, and is humbled in me.

Many people love to sing the hymn "Great Is Thy Faithfulness." Some are surprised to discover the location of the words that form the title and theme of the hymn. Lamentations is not one of the more familiar books of the Bible. And it is, after all, a book filled with laments—expressions of deep sorrow and grief. Many books contain some laments, but this book is the ultimate Book of Lamentations. However, a more positive note is sounded in the middle of the book, a reminder of God's love, which affects the tone of the last half of the book.

The book itself does not name the author. But since ancient times Jeremiah has been considered to be the writer. He had spent his life warning Judah that God was sending judgment on the impenitent people. Other prophets condemned the prophet as a pessimist and a traitor. Jeremiah predicted that Jerusalem would fall to the Babylonians, and he described the terrible destruction that would follow. In 587 B.C. his prophecy came true; however, even Jeremiah was not prepared for the desolation left by the conquerors. His horror and grief are expressed in Lamentations 1:1–3:20. Chapter 1 personifies Jerusalem as a widow in deep mourning. She cried out for passersby to see her sorrow, but no one seemed to care. Chapter 2 acknowledges that God punished Israel. The desperate plight of the city is graphically depicted, including the taunts of the city's enemies. Lamentations 3 has the prophet speaking as a representative of the city. He graphically described God as acting like an enemy of Jerusalem.

Chapter 3:19-20 form the climax of these dark feelings. The difficulties in translating these verses can be seen by comparing translations. The words **remembering** and **remembrance** translate the same word. The word in verse 19 can be a statement "I remember" (NIV) or an imperative "remember" (NASB). The word in verse 20 could have been spoken to people or to God. Most translators apply it to the prophet as he represented Jerusalem ("I remember," NIV) or as a call for others to remember ("remember," NASB). It could have been a call for God to remember—"The memory of my distress and my wanderings is wormwood and gall. Remember, O remember, and stoop down to me" (NEB). A more likely translation of verse 20 is "I well remember them, and my soul is downcast within me" (NIV).

Words such as **affliction** and **misery** show the deep anguish, and words such as **wormwood** and **gall** show the bitterness of their experience. **Wormwood** is a plant with a very bitter taste. **Gall** literally refers to the liver, but it is used figuratively as something bitter. The word **humbled** has the idea of being "downcast" (NIV).

The prophet and survivors were in despair when they saw the ruins of the fallen city. They were as down as people can become. The past reminded them of their sins. The present revealed only misery and woes. The future seemed bleak.

If people live long enough, they can identify with the laments of the city of Jerusalem. We find ourselves with afflictions and bitter experiences. These may be the result of our sins, or they may befall us for reasons we know nothing about.

Lamentations 3:21-24: **This I recall to my mind, therefore have I hope. ²²It is of the LORD's mercies that we are not consumed, because his compassions fail not. ²³They are new every morning: great is thy faithfulness. ²⁴The LORD is my portion, saith my soul; therefore will I hope in him.**

These verses express a different tone. The word **this** in verse 21 refers to what follows, not to what preceded verse 21. Jeremiah had been focusing on remembering the ruin of the city and all that led up to it. Then he recalled something that replaced despair with **hope**. Jeremiah remembered the Lord's promise to return His people after 70 years, and that renewed his grasp on the reality of God's love. In this respect, the Book of Lamentations moved from judgment to hope.

Before the city fell, Jeremiah preached the certainty of judgment. When the end drew near, he preached hope for the future.

Several key words reveal God's love. **Mercies** translates *hesed,* a key Old Testament word for "steadfast love" (NRSV), "great love" (NIV), and "lovingkindness" (NASB). Jeremiah realized that the fact that anyone survived showed God's mercy toward them. Without God's mercy, they would have been **consumed.**

Compassions is another key word for God's love. After commenting on *hesed,* F. B. Huey, Jr. wrote, "Another basis of hope is God's unfailing 'compassions' (*rahamim*; from a word related to the womb, it describes the tender, loving care of a mother), which are experienced in a fresh and new way every day."[1] These expressions of divine compassion **never fail.**

They are new every morning. Like the manna in the wilderness, God's love is new each day. Also like the manna, a person cannot hoard a supply for many days. It must be gathered new every morning. We cannot rely on the momentum of past experiences of God's loving presence. We are grateful for these and we build on them; however, the nature of a personal relationship calls for renewal. What better way to begin the morning than by renewing our experience with our loving God?

Because God's compassions fail not, He is always faithful to His promises. **Great is thy faithfulness.** These words are the title to my favorite hymn. I am grateful that God led Jeremiah to write these words, and that centuries later He guided Thomas O. Chisholm to write the words and William M. Runyan to compose the tune we use to sing this hymn.

> Great is Thy faithfulness, O God, my Father,
> There is no shadow of turning with Thee;
> Thou changest not, Thy compassions, they fail not;
> As Thou hast been, Thou forever wilt be.
> Great is Thy faithfulness! Great is Thy faithfulness!
> Morning by morning new mercies I see;
> All I have needed, Thy hand hath provided;
> Great is Thy faithfulness, Lord, unto me![2]

In the expression **the LORD is my portion,** the word **portion** is used to describe the land given to each tribe. But it came to have a figurative meaning also. It means a treasured possession. "The LORD's portion is his people" (Deut. 32:9). The Lord was the greatest reality in the lives of Jeremiah and the people of God in that day. Their city was in ruins. Nothing in their bleak outward circumstances had changed, but Jeremiah reminded them that in God they had life's most precious treasure. The writer of Psalm 73 went through a time when he envied the wealthy wicked, but God helped him learn that everything without God equals nothing, but God without anything equals everything. The psalmist wrote, "Whom have I in heaven but thee? and there is none upon earth that I desire beside thee. My flesh and my heart faileth: but God is the strength of my heart, and my portion forever" (Ps. 73: 25-26). The psalmist used the same word for **portion** as Jeremiah did.

No matter how terrible the circumstances, remembering and renewing trust in God's goodness and love can encourage God's people. This is true when we realize the troubles are chastisement for sins of God's people—as in Lamentations. It is true when trouble comes for no reason we know—as in the experience of Job. At such times people are tempted to see God as an enemy, but we need to see Him as our Heavenly Father.

What lasting lessons are in Lamentations 3:19-24?

1. When life falls in on us, we are tempted to doubt God's goodness.

2. When we remember God's promises, we can be assured of His love.

3. Being assured of God's love enables us to endure hard times.

4. God's love is constant and true.

God Loves When Others Don't (Luke 19:1-7)

What was the significance of Jesus' visit to Jericho? Why was Zacchaeus so anxious to see Jesus? How did Jesus show God's love to Zacchaeus? Why did the people hate Zacchaeus?

Luke 19:1-4: And Jesus entered and passed through Jericho. ²And, behold, there was a man named Zacchaeus, which was the chief among the publicans, and he was rich. ³And he sought to see Jesus who he was; and could not for the press, because he was little of stature. ⁴And he ran before, and climbed up into a sycamore tree to see him: for he was to pass that way.

Jesus was on His way to Jerusalem (see Luke 18:31-34); therefore, **Jesus entered and passed through Jericho** for the last time. Although **Zacchaeus** didn't know this at the time, this was his last chance to meet Jesus. The Lord was committed to giving His life to save sinners.

Verse 2 introduces **Zacchaeus.** He was **chief among the publicans** ("chief tax collector," HCSB, NIV) in Jericho. This is the only time the word has been found in Greek literature. It is composed of two words: *archi,* "chief," and *telones,* "tax collector."

Jericho was in a strategic location as people entered the land of Israel from the east. One of Jesus' most beloved parables took place on the road between Jericho and Jerusalem (Luke 10:30). Jericho was the first city attacked when Joshua led Israel into the promised land (Josh. 6). It was a thriving center of trade and thus was a city where an enterprising tax collector could become **rich.**

In the Roman system, the privilege of collecting taxes in an area was sold to the highest bidder. In turn, the tax collector had to collect enough taxes to make a profit on his investment. He had the authority of the Roman government behind him in collecting taxes. Such a system was subject to abuse and corruption. Tax collectors were unpopular among the Jewish people. At some point Zacchaeus had chosen to become a tax collector. His name means "righteous one." Perhaps his parents had given him this name in the hope that he would become a good man. At any rate, Zacchaeus chose a way that led to wealth. He had succeeded in amassing a fortune and had become the head of the tax collectors in the area.

Zacchaeus had what most people think will bring the good life. He had money. He had lots of money. Yet in spite of his wealth, he knew something was missing in his life. At that time Jesus was famous throughout the land. Thus when Zacchaeus heard that Jesus was passing through town, **he sought to see Jesus who he was.** We are not told how he had heard about Jesus or what he knew about Him. He knew enough that he wanted to see Jesus. He went to great lengths to catch a glimpse of Jesus. Because Zacchaeus **was little of stature** ("a short man," HCSB, NIV), he was unable to see over the crowd that pressed along the way Jesus was coming. So Zacchaeus **ran before** ("ahead," NIV, HCSB), **and climbed up into a sycamore tree.** That must have been a sight to see. The picture is of this short man running in back of the crowd that lined the street. He could not find a peephole. Then the man ran ahead of the crowd and climbed up a tree with low-hanging branches. Those who saw the city's chief tax collector must have relished the sight. Zacchaeus must have known that everything he was doing exposed him to ridicule, but this did not deter him. This shows the depth of his need.

Luke 19:5-7: **And when Jesus came to the place, he looked up, and saw him, and said unto him, Zacchaeus, make haste, and come down; for today I must abide at thy house. ⁶And he made haste, and came down, and received him joyfully. ⁷And when they saw it, they all murmured, saying, That he was gone to be guest with a man that is a sinner.**

Every eye was on Jesus as He stopped and **looked up.** Those who were near the tree knew Zacchaeus was in that tree. They probably wondered why Jesus stopped at that tree. They must have been surprised when they heard Jesus talking to the little man in the tree. No one was more surprised than Zacchaeus himself. Jesus called him by name. As far as we know, Jesus had never met Jericho's chief tax collector, but He called him by name. This alone was impressive— to realize that the Lord knew Zacchaeus's name. Even more impressive was what Jesus said, **Make haste, and come down; for today I must abide at thy house.** Jesus was often a guest in someone's home, but this is the only record of Jesus inviting Himself. Jesus did not invite Himself merely to have a place to rest. The word **must** reflects a moral and spiritual necessity. Jesus wanted to go to the home of the despised tax collector, and He wanted to go right then.

Zacchaeus spent no time debating how to respond. **He made haste, and came down, and received** ("welcomed," NIV, HCSB) **him joyfully.** Zacchaeus's response was immediate **(made haste)** and joyful **(joyfully).** Jesus had shown His love and the love of the Father by calling Zacchaeus by name and by asking to go into his home. Such concern and acceptance were in total contrast to how others in Jericho treated the chief tax collector. When the crowd **saw** what happened, **they all murmured.** The word **murmured** translates *diagonguzo.* Herschel H. Hobbs wrote, "The very sound of the word is that of humming bees. They kept buzzing angrily among themselves that Jesus would grace the home of this 'sinner.'"³

That **he was gone to be guest with a man that is a sinner** was an accusation often made against Jesus by the Pharisees, who defined just about every non-Pharisee as "a sinner." The criticism in Jericho came from **all** who witnessed Jesus talking with Zacchaeus and entering his house. They all considered the tax collector to be **a sinner.** Jesus knew that Zacchaeus was a sinner, but He had come as the Great Physician to heal sin-sick lives. He was the Good Shepherd who had come to seek and save the lost sheep. Jesus would have agreed that

Zacchaeus was a sinner, but He disagreed with the crowd about how to help sinners. Jesus' strategy was to befriend sinners and call them to receive the loving forgiveness of God.

Zacchaeus is an example of a person whom no one loved. In fact, he seems to have been despised by the people of Jericho. He is portrayed as being alone. No mention is made of family or friends. No one seems to have cared for him but Jesus and the Father, whose love His Son revealed. Millions of people in our world feel alone and unloved. The message of these verses is that God loves all people, including those whom no one else loves.

> Jesus! what a friend for sinners!
> Jesus! lover of my soul;
> Friends may fail me, foes assail me,
> He, my Savior, makes me whole.[4]

What are the lasting lessons in Luke 19:1-7?

1. Some people's goal is to do whatever it takes to make lots of money.
2. Wealth does not satisfy the deepest needs of the human heart.
3. God's love is revealed in the life and death of His Son Jesus.
4. The Lord calls us by name and asks entry into our lives.
5. God loves us when others don't.

God's Love Changes Lives (Luke 19:8-10)

How did Zacchaeus respond to Jesus' visit? Where did the tax collector speak the words of verse 8? What did Jesus mean by His words of verses 9-10?

Luke 19:8-10: And Zacchaeus stood, and said unto the Lord; Behold, Lord, the half of my goods I give to the poor; and if I have taken anything from any man by false accusation, I restore him fourfold. [9]And Jesus said unto him, This day is salvation come to this house, forsomuch as he also is a son of Abraham. [10]For the Son of man is come to seek and to save that which was lost.

The Bible doesn't tell us what went on when Jesus was in Zacchaeus's house. Other famous interviews of Jesus give us some idea of how Jesus may have dealt with him. Also verses 9-10 may provide a clue. Jesus may have shown Zacchaeus how and why he was lost—separated from God and others. Jesus also later spoke of how He had come to seek and save lost people.

Verse 8 contains two important commitments made by Zacchaeus. It is not clear where he spoke these words. Was he alone with Jesus in the house, or had they gone outside where the critical crowd could hear? The word **stood** shows that Zacchaeus was making a formal statement, which implies they were outside. On the other hand, the text says he **said** these words **unto the Lord,** not to the crowd. Thus whether inside or outside, the promise was made to Jesus. However, even if the crowd did not hear the promise, they soon learned of it by what the tax collector did.

The setting for Jesus' words of verses 9-10 is also not spelled out in the text. Personally I have always pictured both of them making their statements after emerging from their conference inside. What Jesus said sounds like an answer to the criticism of the crowd in verse 7. Yet the words of Jesus are introduced with **Jesus said unto him.** Offsetting this, however, is the fact that Jesus used **he,** not "you," when speaking of Zacchaeus. Robert H. Stein wrote, "The statement was made to Zacchaeus, but it was directed to the people because of their reaction in Luke 19:7."[5] Jesus probably spoke to Zacchaeus but loudly enough for the crowd to hear. Whether inside or outside, Jesus spoke these words of acceptance and assurance to and about Jericho's chief tax collector.

Of course, the setting is not as important as the content of what each said. The first part of Zacchaeus's commitment was, **Half of my goods** ("possessions," NIV, HCSB) **I give to the poor. Give** is present tense, but it was not something that Zacchaeus was already doing. It was something he was committing himself to do. "Look, I'll give half of my possessions to the poor" (HCSB). The word for **goods** ("possessions," NIV, HCSB) is the same word in 12:15, "A man's life consisteth not in the abundance of the things which he possesseth."

The second part of Zacchaeus's commitment was his promise to make restitution: **If I have taken anything from any man by false accusation, I restore him fourfold.** The form of the sentence in Greek shows that the word **if** does not imply that there was doubt that he had not done wrong. The sin he had committed was that he had "extorted" (HCSB; "cheated," NIV) more money from some people than they should have paid. The word *sukophanteo,* **by false accusation,** is found only here and in 3:14, where John the Baptist told soldiers what repentance meant for them—"Don't take money from anyone by force or false accusation" (HCSB). The Old Testament Law called for only 20 percent increase in normal cases of restitution, such as accidents (Lev. 6:5; Num. 5:6-7). However, when a sheep was stolen, the guilty person was to make fourfold restitution. For example, when David heard Nathan's story of the rich man who took the poor man's one lamb, David said, "He shall restore the lamb fourfold" (2 Sam. 12:6; see also Ex. 22:1). Thus Zacchaeus was confessing that he had stolen from some people by extortion or fraud.

Since Zacchaeus was giving away **half** his possessions **to the poor,** he had only one-half left from which to make fourfold restitution. If he had extorted a lot of money, Zacchaeus would have to use up all or most of the leftover half making restoration. Jesus had asked the rich young ruler to give everything away; in actual practice Zacchaeus may have ended up doing what the rich young ruler refused to do. Although we do not know how often Zacchaeus had committed extortion, he clearly had done it sometimes.

Jesus' responses in verses 9-10 show how pleased He was with the change in Zacchaeus. Actually the words must also have encouraged the man who had just made a life-changing commitment. The tax collector would probably not receive any encouragement from the people of Jericho, but the words of Jesus brought assurance that he had made the right decisions.

When I read about the change in Zacchaeus, I think of Ebenezer Scrooge, the miser in the story by Charles Dickens. If anyone had told either Scrooge or Zacchaeus that he would soon find joy by giving away his wealth, he would not have believed it.

With the words **this day is salvation come to this house, forsomuch as he also is a son of Abraham,** Jesus emphasized that Zacchaeus was as much an heir of God's promises to Abraham as anyone. By showing God's love for him, Jesus had brought salvation to his house. This after all was Jesus' mission: **to seek and to save that which was lost.** Zacchaeus had been lost. Jesus had sought him and found him. Zacchaeus's response testified to the reality of his salvation. What changed his life? The love of God incarnate in Jesus called him to a new and different way of life. All the criticism of the "good people" of Jericho would only have driven a man like Zacchaeus deeper into sin, but the love in the eyes of the Savior set him on a new path. He saw in the eyes of Jesus not the greedy sinner he had been but the generous person he could become.

What are the lasting lessons in Luke 19:8-10?
1. Experiencing the love of God in Christ will call someone to a new life.
2. Restitution is part of true repentance.
3. Jesus came to seek and to save people who are lost.
4. A transformed life testifies to God's love and power.

❖ *Spiritual Transformations*

In the midst of lamenting the ruin of Jerusalem, Jeremiah remembered God's love and faithfulness. Jesus showed love and concern for Zacchaeus when everyone else despised him. Zacchaeus promised to give half of his possessions to the poor and to make fourfold restitution to anyone from whom he unjustly had taken money.

This lesson is the first in our study of things that encourage us. God's love encourages us when life falls in on us—whether or not we are to blame. His love encourages us by reaching out to us even when no one else does. His love encourages us by changing us into the kind of people who know His joy and peace.

How has God's love helped you in some crisis? _____
How has God loved you when no one else seemed to care? _____
_____
How has God encouraged you by changing your life? _____

Prayer of Commitment: Dear Lord, help me live in the confident assurance of Your love. Amen.

[1]F. B. Huey, Jr., "Jeremiah, Lamentations," in *The New American Commentary*, vol. 16 [Nashville: Broadman Press, 1993], 473.

[2]Thomas O. Chisholm, "Great Is Thy faithfulness," *The Baptist Hymnal* [Nashville: Convention Press, 1991), No. 54.

[3]Herschel H. Hobbs, *An Exposition of the Gospel of Luke* [Grand Rapids: Baker Book House, 1966], 270.

[4]J. Wilbur Chapman, "Jesus! What a Friend for Sinners," No. 185, *The Baptist Hymnal*, 1991.

[5]Robert H. Stein, "Luke," in *The New American Commentary*, vol. 24 [Nashville: Broadman Press, 1992], 468.

ENCOURAGED BY SURE SALVATION

Background Passages: 1 John 3:19-24; 5:1-21
Focal Passages: 1 John 3:23-24; 5:1-5,9-13,18-19
Key Verse: 1 John 5:12

❖ *Significance of the Lesson*

• The *Theme* of this lesson is that believers can be encouraged in knowing that their salvation is sure and settled with God.
• The *Life Question* this lesson addresses is, How can I know I have salvation?
• The *Biblical Truth* is that evidence of salvation includes obedience to God, love for God and His people, belief in the Son of God, and a life changed by God.
• The *Life Impact* is to help you live with the assurance of salvation.
• This is the **Evangelism Lesson** for this quarter.

Can People Know They Have Salvation?

Because of unbelief or indifference, many people aren't concerned about God, sin, salvation, and heaven. Earnest religious people disagree about whether people can know they have eternal life. Some believers consider any such assurance dangerous and presumptuous. The Bible teaches that people who have been saved will be saved in the end. Their perseverance in Christian faith and their lives are evidence that confirms their salvation.

Word Study: *Born of God*

These words, which appear in 1 John 5:1,4,18, refer to the same reality as the new birth of John's Gospel. Jesus described this birth by the Spirit in His famous conversation with Nicodemus (John 3:1-8). God gave to those who received Christ the title "children of God" because they "were born, not of blood, nor of the will of the flesh, nor of the will of man, but of God" (John 1:13).

❖ *Search the Scriptures*

Obedience to the commands of Jesus is evidence that people abide in Christ and He abides in them. People show they love God by loving His children. Those who believe in Christ can know they have eternal life. True Christians live a different kind of life than those under the power of the evil one.

The four outline points answer the Life Question.

Obedience to God (1 John 3:23-24)

*What are some of Christ's **commandments**? How did John use the word **know**? What role of **the Spirit** is mentioned? Why is keeping the commandments a fruit and not the root of salvation?*

3:23-24: And this is his commandment, That we should believe on the name of his Son Jesus Christ, and love one another, as he gave us commandment. ²⁴And he that keepeth his commandments dwelleth in him, and he in him. And hereby we know that he abideth in us, by the Spirit which he hath given us.

This letter is hard to outline. John did not deal in detail with one subject at a time. Instead, he wove his main themes together like a tapestry, which is made up of interwoven threads that together make one picture. Verse 23 begins with two of the main threads that run through the letter: **believe on the name of** God's **Son Jesus Christ, and love one another.** John called these words **his commandment.**

A believer who keeps or obeys the **commandments dwelleth in him, and he in him** ("abides in Him, and He in him," NASB). The word translated **dwelleth** is *meno,* which is translated "abide" in John 15:4. They abide in Christ as the branches abide in the vine. John 15:1-10 elaborates on this point. One evidence of abiding in Christ is obedience to His commands. Bearing the fruit of obedience does not save people; however, bearing the fruit of obedience is evidence of the life-giving relationship of abiding in Christ. This is an important point in this lesson. We are not saved by obedience but by knowing the One who gave Himself for us. However, our obedience confirms the relationship.

Three groups can be identified. A large number of people think that living a good life can save them. They think they can obey God's laws in their own strength. They are wrong. Only by God's grace can anyone be saved. Then obedience is possible. Another group thinks they can ensure themselves a place in heaven by professing faith, but they fail to do God's will. When faith is real, people should publicly profess it. However, Jesus condemned those whose profession of faith does not lead to an obedient life: "Not every one that saith unto me, Lord, Lord, shall enter into the kingdom of heaven; but he that doeth the will of my Father which is in heaven" (Matt. 7:21). The third group are genuine believers who show by their obedience that they have a right relation with the Lord. Obedience is the fruit, not the root, of a saving relation with the Lord.

The word **know** is found throughout 1 John. Two Greek words were translated **know** in 1 John. The word *ginosko,* which is in verse 24, appears 25 times in 1 John. *Ginosko* is used to describe knowing God or Christ (2:13-14). At other times it is used to describe something people know to be true. When used in this way it can be translated "are sure." The word appears in both ways in 1 John 2:3: "We do know that we know him," or as the *Holman Christian Standard Bible* reads, "We are sure that we have come to know Him."

Verse 24 contains the first reference to **the Spirit.** In actual practice, abiding in Christ is the same reality as living with His Spirit within us and guiding us. There were many spirits. How can Christians discern when someone is led by the Holy Spirit? When the Spirit is within, a person's life resembles the life of Jesus by bearing the fruit of the Spirit, not by doing the works of the flesh (Gal. 5:19-23).

What are the lasting lessons in 1 John 3:23-24?

1. Abiding in Christ is the basis for knowing that we are saved.
2. Obeying the Lord is the fruit, not the root, of salvation.

Love for God and His People (1 John 5:1-5)

*How do people become **children of God**? What are the evidences that people have been **born of God**? Why is loving other believers evidence of eternal security? Why do God's commandments seem **grievous** to some people? What kind of faith overcomes the world?*

5:1-5: Whosoever believeth that Jesus is the Christ is born of God: and every one that loveth him that begat loveth him also that is begotten of him. ²By this we know that we love the children of God, when we love God, and keep his commandments. ³For this is the love of God, that we keep his commandments: and his commandments are not grievous. ⁴For whatsoever is born of God

overcometh the world: and this is the victory that overcometh the world, even our faith. **⁵Who is he that overcometh the world, but he that believeth that Jesus is the Son of God?**

In each of our blocks of Focal Verses, we need to distinguish the basis for assurance from evidences that confirm that we have eternal life. Being **born of God** is one way of stating the basis for our assurance. (See the Word Study.) Jesus told Nicodemus that a new birth was necessary in order to see the kingdom of God. This new birth is the new life that begins when the Spirit comes into a life. It is more than God giving us another chance to do better. It is a totally different life made possible by the Spirit.

John's point is that those who are **born of God** become **children of God.** John made two points about what this means in our relationships. For one thing, this means that children of God love their Heavenly Father. Second, it means that we love others who also are children of God: **Every one that loveth him that begat loveth him also that is begotten of him** ("every one who loves the parent also loves his child," HCSB; "whoever loves the Father loves the child born of Him," NASB). Loving fellow believers is one line of evidence that confirms our assurance that we are children of God. An earlier passage makes this point clearly: "We know that we have passed from death unto life, because we love the brethren. He that loveth not his brother abideth in death" (3:14). This offers confirming evidence of eternal life to those who love fellow believers, and it casts doubt on the salvation of a professing believer who does not love fellow Christians.

As in 3:23-24, these are called God's **commandments.** John wrote that **his commandments are not grievous** ("not burdensome," NIV; "not a burden," HCSB). This is a point where many non-Christians misunderstand Christianity. They think Christianity is a heavy burden. Perhaps they get this from the strained expressions of the faces of some Christians. We too can lose sight of God's grace and power. We are in touch with that power through **our faith.** Such faith makes possible **the victory that overcometh the world.**

We are looking at these verses to emphasize that love for God and other believers is one kind of evidence that we are children of God. Do you love to be with fellow Christians? Do you enjoy worshiping, learning, and serving together in and through the church? Something is seriously wrong if a professing Christian can't answer yes to both these questions.

What are the lasting lessons in 1 John 5:1-5?
1. Being born of God makes us children of God forever.
2. Evidence of being God's children is love for the Father and for brothers and sisters in Christ.

Belief in the Son of God (1 John 5:9-13)

How has God borne testimony to His Son? What basic message was God sending in His Son? What is saving faith? How does verse 13 summarize the doctrine of assurance?

5:9-12: If we receive the witness of men, the witness of God is greater: for this is the witness of God which he hath testified of his Son. [10]He that believeth on the Son of God hath the witness in himself: he that believeth not God hath made him a liar; because he believeth not the record that God gave of his Son. [11]And this is the record, that God hath given to us eternal life, and this life is in his Son. [12]He that hath the Son hath life; and he that hath not the Son of God hath not life.

God bore **witness** or testimony to Jesus as **his Son.** God also uses **the witness of men,** but what God testified concerning Jesus **is greater.** The Gospels record many ways in which the Father testified concerning His Son's nature and mission—from the announcement of His birth through His victory over the grave. In essence, the Word of God contain His testimonies to His Son. Some believe the testimonies, and others don't. Those who believe receive an inner confirmation when they not only believe the facts but also believe **on the Son of God.** Those who refuse to believe even the biblical record make God seem to be **a liar.**

What is the overall message or **record**? John had the ability to state the deepest truths in ways people can understand. Verse 11 illustrates this skill. He summed up **the record** like this: **God hath given to us eternal life, and this life is in his Son.** In John's writings **eternal life** is emphasized. This life is the life of those born of God's Spirit. It is a different kind of life than just being alive, but both physical life and eternal life are gifts of God. Eternal life begins when a person trusts Jesus as Savior, and it never ends.

Who has this eternal life? Verse 12 states the answer in a way no one could fail to grasp: **He that hath the Son hath life; and he that hath not the Son hath not life.** Years ago I had the privilege of being a counselor at two of Billy Graham's crusades. Counselors were trained to use certain Bible verses in talking with a person who came forward. These verses from 1 John 5:11-12 were used to help see the reality and security of saving faith. The counselor used a tract and a Bible. The Bible represented the Son of God. The tract represented eternal life. Then the tract (eternal life) was placed inside the Bible (the Son) to illustrate verse 11. This signified that eternal life was in the Son of God. Finally, the Bible was offered to the person who came forward. When the person took the Bible containing the tract, that illustrated verse 12. By laying hold of Jesus, one receives the life that is in Him.

5:13: These things have I written unto you that believe on the name of the Son of God; that ye may know that ye have eternal life, and that ye may believe on the name of the Son of God.

This is a key verse on the certainty of eternal life for Christians. Bible students compare this statement of purpose to the stated purpose of John's Gospel (John 20:30-31). John wrote his Gospel so people might have life through believing in Jesus Christ as the Son of God. John wrote this letter so believers in Jesus Christ can **know that** they **have eternal life.**

John obviously was convinced that true believers can and should know they have eternal life. We already have noted that some people trust in a profession of faith, which proves bogus because they continue to live in sin and fail to do the will of God. We need to be sure that the faith we profess is saving faith. John also was concerned about those who denied that Jesus is the eternal Son of God who became human in order to reveal God and to save sinners. Many people today do not accept biblical truths about Jesus, and thus they have no basis for exercising saving faith. Others have correct intellectual beliefs about Jesus; yet they never commit themselves to the Lord. True Christians believe what the Bible says about Jesus, and they have made a personal commitment to Him.

Verse 13 says that saving faith is to **believe on the name of the Son of God.** In English we have no verb form for the noun *faith*. Therefore, we must use the verb *believe*, which has the connotation of cognitive assent. People can have orthodox *beliefs* but fail to exercise personal *faith* in Christ. They can *believe* that what the Bible says about Jesus is true, but they receive salvation and eternal life only when they *entrust* themselves to Jesus as their personal Lord and Savior.

What are the lasting lessons in 1 John 5:9-13?

1. People ought to believe God's testimony to His Son.

2. Those who have the Son have eternal life; the rest do not have such life.

3. Christians can and should know they have eternal life.

4. Saving faith is commitment to and trust in Jesus Christ.

Life Changed by God (1 John 5:18-19)

Do Christians ever sin? What are two ways of translating the last part of verse 18? What is meant by "perseverance of the saints"?

5:18-19: We know that whosoever is born of God sinneth not; but he that is begotten of God keepeth himself, and that wicked one toucheth him not. ¹⁹And we know that we are of God, and the whole world lieth in wickedness.

Some translations of verse 18 seem to contradict 1 John 1:8,10. That is, **Whosoever is born of God sinneth not** seems to contradict, "If we say that we have no sin, we deceive ourselves, and the truth is not in us" (1:8). The true meaning of these verses depends on understanding how to translate the verbs for committing sin. Unfortunately some translations use a tense of the verb that can refer to any single sin. Other translations use a tense that describes continuous action— "We know that anyone born of God does not continue to sin" (NIV). You can see what a difference there is between the meanings of these two translations. If John had been referring to a single sin, he would have been claiming that true children of God are perfect—without any sin of any kind. If John had been referring to living in sin as a way of life, he was saying that while Christians are not yet perfect they do not live a sinful life. The latter view is consistent with the rest of 1 John and the entire New Testament.

The last part of verse 18 has another translation issue. In Greek there is only one letter difference between the words **himself** *(eauton)* and "him" *(auton),* but that slight difference results in two different meanings. The *King James Version* reads, **he that is begotten of God keepeth himself.** This translation assumes John meant that a child of God keeps himself living for Christ. Other translations follow manuscripts with the alternative reading. The *New American Standard Bible* reads, "He who was born of God keeps him" ("the One who is born of God keeps him," HCSB; "the one who was born of God keeps him safe," NIV; "God's own Son protects them," CEV). The meaning is that Christ keeps one of His own. Actually, both meanings are taught elsewhere in Scripture. The first is the doctrine of the *perseverance* of the saints. The second can be called the *preservation* of the saints. True believers *persevere* because they are *preserved* by the Lord.

Whether we speak of perseverance of the saints or preservation by the Lord, neither leads to presumption. Presumption is false confidence that we can live as we please and God will not punish us. At times someone tells me about a person who once seemed to be a Christian but who now lives like non-Christians. The questioner asks, "Is he saved or lost?" My usual response is: "I don't know, but one of two things is true. Either the person never was truly saved, or the person is seriously out of fellowship with God. In either case, the person is in a dangerous spiritual plight."

Living for the God to whom we belong isn't easy when **the whole world lieth in wickedness** ("is under the sway of the evil one," HCSB). But because of the preservation by the Lord resulting in the perseverance of the saints the **wicked one toucheth him not** ("the evil one does not touch him," HCSB; "the evil one cannot harm him," NIV; "the devil cannot harm them," CEV).

Perseverance of the saints is based on the preservation of the saints by God's grace and power. *The Baptist Faith and Message*, 2000, states: "All true believers endure to the end. Those whom God has accepted in Christ, and sanctified by His Spirit, will never fall away from the state of grace, but shall persevere to the end. Believers may fall into sin through neglect and temptation, whereby they grieve the Spirit, impair their graces and comforts, and bring reproach on the cause of Christ and temporal judgments on themselves; yet they shall be kept by the power of God through faith unto salvation."[1]

True faith doesn't lead to sinful living; rather, assurance of salvation motivates our best as we live in faith and hope. The assurance that we will be like Jesus (1 John 3:3) does not lead to presuming we will be saved no matter how we live. Instead, it calls us to seek to become like Him now.

What are the lasting lessons in 1 John 5:18-19?

1. Those who have been born anew do not live a sinful life.

2. Those who have been born anew persevere in faith because they are preserved by Christ.

3. *Perseverance* is based on *preservation*, but it does not lead to *presumption*.

❖ Spiritual Transformations

The Focal Verses in this lesson focus on four marks of persons who are genuine Christians. They obey divine commandments. They show they are God's children by loving one another. They know they have eternal life because they have committed themselves to Jesus Christ. And as children of God, they persevere in a transformed life by the preserving power of Christ.

> I steadier step when I recall
> That, if I slip, Thou dost not fall.[2]

If you should die today, do you know that you would go to heaven?

_____

If your answer is no, you need to trust Jesus as your personal Savior. _____

If your answer is yes, what difference is this assurance making in you now? _____

Prayer of Commitment: Lord, I am grateful that through Jesus Christ I know I have eternal life. Amen.

[1] *The Baptist Faith and Message*, 2000, "God's Purpose of Grace," Article V.

[2] Arthur Hugh Clough, "With Whom Is No Variableness, Neither Shadow of Turning," in *Masterpieces of Religious Verse*, edited by James Dalton Morrison [New York: Harper & Brothers Publishers, 1948], 39.

ENCOURAGED BY
REDEMPTIVE USEFULNESS

Background Passage: Nehemiah 1:1–2:18
Focal Passages: Nehemiah 1:2-7,10-11; 2:4-8,17-18
Key Verse: Nehemiah 1:11

❖ *Significance of the Lesson*

• The *Theme* of this lesson is that we can be encouraged in knowing that God can use us, regardless of our past or present circumstances.
• The *Life Question* this lesson addresses is, How can I be useful when I feel so useless?
• The *Biblical Truth* is that the Lord can use anyone who depends on Him, regardless of circumstances, including distance, opposition, or one's position in life.
• The *Life Impact* is to help you live as a useful servant of God.

Useful or Useless?

Many people feel they are useless to God or to anyone else. They are acutely aware of their limitations, shortcomings, past failures, and unfavorable circumstances. Some are so overwhelmed by people's needs that they don't try to meet any of them. Scripture shows that God can use anyone who relies on His guidance and strength.

Word Study: *Mercy*

The word **mercy** in Nehemiah 1:11 translates the Hebrew word *racham*. This word can be translated "favor" (NIV) and "compassion" (NASB). The same word appears in Nehemiah 9:19,27,28,31 and in Psalm 51:1.

❖ Search the Scriptures

Jerusalem had no walls. Nehemiah learned of the plight of his disheartened people. Deeply disturbed, he confessed his own sins and the sins of the people. As the king of Persia's cupbearer, Nehemiah had access to the king. He asked God to cause the king to be open to his request for help. Prayerfully, Nehemiah went to the king and asked permission to go to the city of his forefathers. After traveling to Jerusalem, Nehemiah inspected the ruined walls, proposed that the people rebuild the walls, and promised that God would be with them. The people committed themselves to the task.

The five outline points answer the Life Question.

Assess the Situation (Neh. 1:2-3)

Why did Nehemiah ask about the returned exiles? Why were walls needed for Jerusalem?

1:2-3: **That Hanani, one of my brethren, came, he and certain men of Judah; and I asked them concerning the Jews that had escaped, which were left of the captivity, and concerning Jerusalem. ³And they said unto me, The remnant that are left of the captivity there in the province are in great affliction and reproach: the wall of Jerusalem also is broken down, and the gates thereof are burned with fire.**

Nehemiah is the main character in the Book of Nehemiah. Large portions of the book are written in the first person. Nehemiah 1–7 and 12:31–13:31 constitute the so-called Nehemiah Memoirs. Verse 1 introduces "the words of Nehemiah." The time was "the twentieth year" of King Artaxerxes I [ahr-tuh-ZUHRK-seez] of Persia (2:1). The years of his reign were 464-424 B.C. Thus the year was 445 B.C. Nehemiah was in Shushan (Susa) in the winter palace of the Persian kings, where he served as cupbearer to the king (1:11). Although he was a Jew, he held this high office in the king's service.

During that time Nehemiah was visited by some people from Judah. Nehemiah called **Hanani** [huh-NAY-nigh], **one of my brethren.** This could refer to a real brother or to a fellow Jew; however, because Hanani is mentioned in 7:2, he was probably a brother. With him were **certain men of Judah.** Nehemiah **asked them concerning the Jews that had escaped, which were left of the captivity.** The first part of verse 3 is equally ambiguous: **the remnant that are left of the**

captivity there in the province. This could refer to the Jews who were left when others went into captivity. More likely, however, he was referring to those who went into exile and whose descendants had now returned to Judah ("the Jewish remnant that survived the exile . . . those who survived the exile and are back in the province," NIV). In other words, Nehemiah inquired about the welfare of the Jews in Judah at that time. It was like asking, "How are the folks back home in Judah?"

The report on conditions in Judah was not good. The people were **in great affliction and reproach** ("in great trouble and disgrace," NIV). The source of their plight was that **the wall of Jerusalem** was **broken down, and the gates thereof** were **burned with fire.** The Babylonian king Nebuchadnezzar [neb-yoo-kad-NEZ-uhr] had destroyed the wall and burned the gates in 587 B.C., over a century and a half earlier. Ezra 4:7-23 describes a recent attempt to rebuild the wall. Enemies of the Jews thwarted this work. These enemies reported to King Artaxerxes what the Jews were doing. They accused the Jews of planning a revolt against Persian rule. The king ordered that work on the wall stop. The enemies probably came and destroyed the work that had been done.

Regardless of when the wall and gates were destroyed, the city was in danger and the people under reproach. In those days a city without a wall was wide open to the attacks of enemies. The reproach was felt because their God seemed to have left them in this vulnerable condition. Hanani and the others reported this plight to Nehemiah, when he inquired about conditions in Judah. Nehemiah probably knew something of the need, but this description showed how desperate the need was.

We live in a world of all kinds of needs. Anyone who wants to be useful to God and others will see needs that someone can meet. One danger of assessing the situation in which we live is that we may become so overwhelmed by the number and complexity of the needs that we throw up our hands in frustration. As a consequence, we may do nothing. Or we can follow the example of Nehemiah.

What are the lasting lessons in Nehemiah 1:2-3?

1. Our world is filled with needs of all kinds.
2. God's people ought to be aware of these needs.

Confess Sin (Neh. 1:4-7)

What words show Nehemiah's concern? What were the characteristics of his prayer?

1:4-7: And it came to pass, when I heard these words, that I sat down and wept, and mourned certain days, and fasted, and prayed before the God of heaven, ⁵and said, I beseech thee, O LORD God of heaven, the great and terrible God, that keepeth covenant and mercy for them that love him and observe his commandments: ⁶Let thine ear now be attentive, and thine eyes open, that thou mayest hear the prayer of thy servant, which I pray before thee now, day and night, for the children of Israel thy servants, and confess the sins of the children of Israel, which we have sinned against thee: both I and my father's house have sinned. ⁷We have dealt very corruptly against thee, and have not kept the commandments, nor the statutes, nor the judgments, which thou commandedst thy servant Moses.

Verse 4 shows Nehemiah's response to his awareness of this need. Notice the words in verse 4 that describe what he did: **sat down . . . wept . . . wept . . . mourned . . . fasted . . . prayed.** Notice also that he continued to do this for **days.** These were actions of a person who had heard about a need that caused him great concern. He deeply cared about the plight of his fellow Jews although he was many miles from the site of the needs.

Verses 5-11 record a prayer of Nehemiah during these days of concern. It is significant that Nehemiah began with prayer. One theme of the early chapters of the Book of Nehemiah is that the hand of the Lord was with Nehemiah. Nehemiah knew that this great need could only be met by God's guidance and strength.

The prayer reveals some characteristics of true prayer. The most important aspect of prayer is the God to whom we pray. Verse 5 gives the titles of the One to whom Nehemiah prayed. He is the **LORD God of heaven.** Because He is God of heaven, He is **great** beyond all definitions of great. He also is **terrible** ("awesome," NIV). Because He is the **LORD,** the personal name of Israel's God, He "keeps his covenant of love with those who love him and obey his commands" (NIV).

Nehemiah asked God to **hear** and answer his **prayer.** He was praying **day and night.** This need not mean that Nehemiah prayed 24 hours each day; but since it was combined with fasting, Nehemiah's prayer was made many times throughout the day and night. The Bible teaches us to keep on praying. This is not necessary to impress God but in order that He can prepare us for living for Him. Another reason we keep praying is that real needs are constantly on our minds and hearts.

Nehemiah's was an intercessory prayer, not just a personal petition. He was thinking of the people in Jerusalem. He prayed that God would show mercy to His sinful people. He confessed **the sins of the children of Israel.** Nehemiah included himself and his family among those who had **sinned.** He stated, **Both I and my father's house have sinned.** This shows two things. For one thing, being right with God spiritually is the most important need of every person. The people of Jerusalem needed a new wall, but their basic need was to be the kind of people who honored the Lord. The other thing it shows is that the one doing the praying must be right with God. Thus Jesus taught us to pray, "Forgive us our sins" (Luke 11:4).

Nehemiah 1:7 refers to Israel's past history of continually disobeying God's commandment. More of Nehemiah's prayer will be considered under the next heading of the lesson.

In this world of needs, God is seeking people whom He can use to help meet each need. He laid on Nehemiah's heart Jerusalem's need for walls. He will lay on our hearts some need that we can help meet. Our first response should be to pray earnestly about the need. We need to pray for the spiritual needs of those who are involved, and we need to confess our own sins and be sure our hearts are open to the Lord.

What are the lasting lessons in Nehemiah 1:4-7?

1. Seeing needs should cause concern that the needs be met.
2. Praying is the place to begin in seeking to meet needs.

Petition God (Neh. 1:10-11)

*To what event does verse 10 refer? What did Nehemiah mean by **the prayer of thy servants**? What did he mean by **prosper**? Whose **mercy** was Nehemiah seeking? What was the role of **the king's cupbearer**?*

1:10-11: Now these are thy servants and thy people, whom thou hast redeemed by thy great power, and by thy strong hand. ¹¹O Lord, I beseech thee, let now thine ear be attentive to the prayer of thy servant, and to the prayer of thy servants, who desire to fear thy name: and prosper, I pray thee, thy servant this day, and grant him mercy in the sight of this man. For I was the king's cupbearer.

Nehemiah's prayer continues in verses 8-11. Verse 8 refers to God's warning to ancient Israel that disobedience would be punished by being scattered among the nations. Verse 9 refers to God's promise of restoration to His people. Verse 10 describes how the Lord **redeemed His people by** His **great power.** This could refer to the redemption of Israel from Egyptian slavery, or it could refer to His sending them from exile to the promised land. Verse 11 repeats much of verse 6 by asking the Lord to **be attentive to the prayer of thy servant, and to the prayer of thy servants.**

Nehemiah prayed that he might **prosper** and that God would **grant him mercy in the sight of this man** ("Give your servant success today by granting him favor in the presence of this man," NIV). The next verses make clear that **this man** was King Artaxerxes I. At some point in the process of learning about the need, being concerned about it, and praying about it, Nehemiah began to hear God's call to take a leadership position in rebuilding the wall of Jerusalem. This is implied by the prayer that God give him favor in the king's eyes, and it is made clear by the events that followed.

As Nehemiah prayed, a specific day (**this day,** "today," NIV) came when he intended to go to the king with the request that he be allowed to go to Jerusalem. He asked God to give him success in this mission. He asked God to cause the king to approve him and his request. Going into the presence of a Persian king was dangerous. Persian kings were fickle in how they responded to such requests. Nehemiah also knew that the king had earlier ordered that the Jews' attempt to rebuild the wall be stopped.

However, Nehemiah had two reasons for cautious optimism. One was that he **was the king's cupbearer.** In some countries this post was held by some expendable servant whose main job was to taste a small portion of what the king ate and drank to ensure that it was not poisoned. But "recent studies have shown the importance of this position. In the ancient Near Eastern court the cupbearer, with his direct access to the king, was regarded as important and influential."[1] Some sources consider the cupbearer as second only to the king. Thus when Nehemiah later was named governor of Judah (5:14), this was in a sense a demotion. This direct access was probably a key factor in Nehemiah's sense of call.

The other reason for Nehemiah to be optimistic is even more important. He felt that he was doing what God wanted him to do. His trust was not in his position or abilities but in the Lord. Nehemiah knew that the king—for all his power—was only a man. God is the Lord of all—including kings. Later Nehemiah testified that all that happened in leading him to Jerusalem was the hand of the Lord.

Becoming concerned enough about some need and praying for God to meet that need led Nehemiah to hear God calling him to be God's instrument in meeting that need. Praying can be dangerous. Jesus told the apostles to pray that the Lord of the harvest send workers into the fields (Matt. 9:38). A few verses later we read, "These twelve Jesus sent forth" (10:5). Do you really want to be useful to God? Look about you at the needs. Pray about the needs, and you will find your place in meeting needs.

What are the lasting lessons of Nehemiah 1:10-11?

1. Becoming concerned enough to pray about some need often leads to a call to do something about meeting the need.

2. God sometimes places us in places and situations that enable us to meet certain needs.

Enlist Support (Neh. 2:4-8)

Why did Nehemiah go to the king? How did he present his requests? How did the king respond? How did Nehemiah express his faith in the Lord's leadership?

2:4-8: Then the king said unto me, For what dost thou make request? So I prayed to the God of heaven. ⁵And I said unto the king, If it please the king, and if thy servant have found favor in thy sight, that thou wouldest send me unto Judah, unto the city of my fathers' sepulchers, that I may build it. ⁶And the king said unto me, (the queen also sitting by him,) For how long shall thy journey be? and when wilt thou return? So it pleased the king to send me; and I set him a time. ⁷Moreover I said unto the king, If it please the king, let letters be given me to the governors beyond the river, that they may convey me over till I come into Judah; ⁸and a letter unto Asaph the keeper of the king's forest, that he may give me timber to make beams for the gates of the palace which appertained to the house, and for the wall of the city, and for the house that I shall enter into. And the king granted me, according to the good hand of my God upon me.

Hanani's visit was in the month of Chisleu [KISS-loo] (Neh. 1:1; "Kislev," NIV), which spans parts of November-December. He presented the matter to the king in the month of Nisan (2:1). "Since

'Nisan' spans parts of our March-April, four months had passed since Nehemiah received news from Jerusalem. He had been praying and planning during these four months so that he would be ready when the opportunity arose."[2]

Nehemiah's opportunity came on a day when the king asked his cupbearer why he looked so sad. This was unusual for Nehemiah, so the king felt Nehemiah was depressed about something. Although he had prayed for just such an opportunity, Nehemiah was afraid of the king's reaction when he made his request; but he spoke up. He said that the city where his forefathers were buried had no gates (2:1-3).

Nehemiah was relieved when the king asked, **For what dost thou make request?** "What is it you want?" (NIV). Before answering, Nehemiah **prayed to the God of heaven.** "Nehemiah had prayed for months, but he knew he was completely dependent on God's work in the king's heart at this moment."[3] Nehemiah used the appropriate words of respect for the king. He began his request by saying, **If it please the king, and if thy servant have found favor in thy sight.** In 1:11 Nehemiah had prayed that the king would show mercy to him. As he presented his request, Nehemiah said he hoped his words would please the king. These words led up to the heart of his request: **Send me unto Judah, unto the city of my fathers' sepulchers, that I may build it** ("rebuild it," NIV). Nehemiah again carefully avoided naming the city of Jerusalem, which in the king's mind might still have had negative overtones.

The kings' questions show he was kindly disposed toward the request: **For how long shall thy journey be? and when wilt thou return?** "How long will your journey take, and when will you get back?" (NIV). Encouraged by this positive response, Nehemiah **set him a time,** although verse 6 does not tell how long. As the rest of the book shows, Nehemiah probably returned to report to the king, but he did not resume his former duties as the king's cupbearer. Instead, Nehemiah became governor of Judah.

Nehemiah had shown courage and faith in making the request to be authorized to go and rebuild the walls of his native city. Encouraged by the king's favorable response to his basic request, he made the additional requests of verses 7-8. Nehemiah had received permission to go, but he knew he would need protection on the way and materials with which to build. Only the king could provide these. Therefore Nehemiah

asked for **letters . . . to the governors beyond the river.** Nehemiah
was referring to the large area on the other side of the Euphrates
River from Persia. Nehemiah would need to pass through many
provinces on his trip from Persia to Jerusalem. The **letters** instructed
the governors to **convey me over** ("provide me safe-conduct," NIV) **till
I come into Judah.** These letters would help ensure a safe journey.

Nehemiah also boldly requested **a letter unto Asaph** [AY-saf] **the
keeper of the king's forest.** Nehemiah needed **timber** for three con-
structions: (1) **the gates of the palace which appertained to the
house** ("the gates of the citadel by the temple," NIV); (2) **the wall of
the city**; and (3) Nehemiah's own **house** ("residence," NIV).

The king **granted** all Nehemiah's requests. Looking back on the last
four months, Nehemiah attributed the king's positive response **to the
good hand of my God upon me.** He did not attribute his success thus
far to his skills as a negotiator, nor did he give the credit to the king's
good nature or his high regard for his cupbearer. These played a part
in what happened, but Nehemiah gave the glory to God. He had felt he
was doing what God wanted him to do. Now he felt even greater confidence this was the work of God. He realized that all kinds of difficulties and dangers lay ahead. The task of rebuilding the walls while
surrounded by enemies sounded impossible, but he moved ahead
because the good hand of his God was leading in this task.

What are the lasting lessons in Nehemiah 2:4-8?

1. Pray before, during, and after undertaking some task for the
Lord.

2. Be bold in asking for help from others.

3. Praise the Lord for His good hand on you and on others.

Encourage Others (Neh. 2:17-18)

*How did Nehemiah challenge the people of Jerusalem to begin
rebuilding the city's wall? How did they respond?*

**2:17-18: Then said I unto them, Ye see the distress that we are
in, how Jerusalem lieth waste, and the gates thereof are burned
with fire: come, and let us build up the wall of Jerusalem, that we
be no more a reproach. ¹⁸Then I told them of the hand of my God
which was good upon me; as also the king's words that he had
spoken unto me. And they said, Let us rise up and build. So they
strengthened their hands for this good work.**

After making the long journey to Jerusalem, Nehemiah did not reveal his mission right away. He knew that this task would require everyone working together. With only a few men accompanying him, Nehemiah rode around the city's broken walls by night. He wanted to see for himself the condition. Only after making this inspection did he call together the leaders and workers of the city. He began his challenge by reminding them of **the distress that we are in.** Notice that Nehemiah used **we** to show them that he felt he was one of them. He reminded them that **Jerusalem lieth waste, and the gates thereof are burned with fire.** They surely knew this, but they had become so accustomed to the situation that they had given up hope of doing anything about it. Many remembered the failure of their earlier effort to rebuild the wall.

Nehemiah had carefully planned how to challenge the leaders to action. His basic challenge was, **Come, and let us build up the wall of Jerusalem.** Notice he said **us.** He reminded them of the **reproach** heaped on them because their city had no wall. This reflected badly on them and on their God. "The wall itself was more than a protection for Jerusalem and its citizens. Its condition at the time was symbolic of the low esteem in which the Jews were held by their neighbors. Moreover, it was a reflection on the status of their religion in the eyes of surrounding peoples."[4]

Nehemiah's testimony assured them of two reasons to undertake this task. First, he testified of **the hand of my God which was good upon me** ("I also told them about the gracious hand of my God upon me," NIV). He probably recounted the events described up to this point in the book. Second, he told them of **the king's words.** This reassured them that King Artaxerxes now approved a project that he earlier had stopped. Obviously, this was a stirring call for commitment. Each person had to choose individually, and they all needed to commit themselves to work together. Rebuilding the wall and gates would be an involved process with many aspects and tasks; however, Nehemiah wanted them to keep their overall goal in mind.

Those who heard the challenge responded using the words of the challenge: **Let us rise up and build** ("Let us start rebuilding," NIV). **So they strengthened their hands for this good work** is a fairly literal translation of the Hebrew, but the meaning is not completely clear. This has led to several ways to translate their words: "So they began this good work," NIV; "So they got everything ready," CEV; "So they committed themselves to the common good," NRSV; "They set about the work vigorously and to good purpose," NEB, REB. Charles Fensham suggested, "So they encouraged themselves for the good cause."[5] Nehemiah had been encouraged by the Lord's good hand on him, and God used him in turn to challenge and encourage the people. Each one made his own decision, but they encouraged one another. All of them were encouraged to be given a useful task by God.

What are the lasting lessons of Nehemiah 2:17-18?

1. God uses others to remind us of serious needs.

2. Some needs can be met by one person, but many needs require the commitment and work of a number of people.

3. God will help people do what He has led them to do.

❖ *Spiritual Transformations*

Nehemiah became aware of Jerusalem's need for a new wall. He was so concerned that he prayed earnestly and continually. He asked God to cause the king to respond positively to his requests. He went boldly to the king and received all he asked for. Then he went to Jerusalem, where his challenge was received positively.

Nehemiah could have found many excuses for not taking each step. He could have said things such as: "The task is too big for me. Besides I live many miles away." "God can find someone better qualified than I am." "The king has already stopped such a project before." "I don't have the resources needed for such a huge task." "I am a stranger to the people of Jerusalem." However, rather than making excuses, Nehemiah moved ahead one step at a time until the task was done.

What do you do that makes you feel useful to the Lord? _____

_____

What need is God calling you to meet? _____
How have you responded? _____

Prayer of Commitment: Lord, make my life useful to You. Amen.

[1]F. Charles Fensham, *The Books of Ezra and Nehemiah*, in The New International Commentary on the Old Testament [Grand Rapids: William B. Eerdmans Publishing Company, 1982), 157.

[2]Mervin Breneman, "Ezra, Nehemiah, Esther," in *The New American Commentary*, vol. 10 [Nashville: Broadman & Holman Publishers, 1993], 174.

[3]Breneman, "Ezra, Nehemiah, Esther," NAC, 176.

[4]Jacob M. Myers, *Ezra—Nehemiah*, in The Anchor Bible [Garden City: Doubleday & Company, Inc., 1965], 105.

[5]Fensham, *The Books of Ezra and Nehemiah*, 168.

ENCOURAGED BY FAITHFUL HOPE

Background Passage: Habakkuk 1–3
Focal Passages: Habakkuk 1:2-6,12-13; 2:2-4,18-20; 3:17-19a
Key Verse: Habakkuk 2:20

❖ *Significance of the Lesson*

• The *Theme* of this lesson is that we can be encouraged in knowing that God offers us hope in the midst of a violent world.
• The *Life Question* this lesson addresses is, Where can I find hope in the midst of violence and injustice?
• The *Biblical Truth* is that the righteous person who lives by faith can have hope in God regardless of the human and natural circumstances around him.
• The *Life Impact* is to help you live with hope in God.

A World of Violence and Injustice

Terrorism. War. Child abduction. Natural disaster. Corporate scandal. Many people wonder where God can be in such a world. Some conclude that such circumstances show that God—if there is a God—must be either powerless or indifferent. The biblical view of God, however, affirms that God works for good in such a world. God may not act the way believers want Him to act; but they can have confident hope in Him, regardless of the circumstances about them.

Word Study: *Violence*

The Hebrew word *hamas*, rendered **violence** in Habakkuk 1:2-3, denotes wrong and harm, both physical and ethical. It is closely related to the causes of violence—injustice, lying, and oppression. The word describes one of the main sins before the great flood (Gen. 6:11,13). Violence was condemned by many of the prophets, including Habakkuk's contemporary Jeremiah (6:7; 20:8).

❖ *Search the Scriptures*

Habakkuk [huh-BAK-kuk] asked God why He allowed sins of injustice and violence in the land. God revealed that He was going to send the Chaldeans [kal-DEE-uhns] to chastise His wayward people. This led Habakkuk to ask how God could allow a godless nation to defeat His own nation. Habakkuk wrote that God's people live by faith. He testified that he would rejoice in the Lord regardless of what happened.

Violence Abounds (Hab. 1:2-4)

What questions did Habakkuk ask God? What sins did he mention?
1:2-4: O Lord, how long shall I cry, and thou wilt not hear! even cry out unto thee of violence, and thou wilt not save! ³Why dost thou show me iniquity, and cause me to behold grievance? for spoiling and violence are before me: and there are that raise up strife and contention. ⁴Therefore the law is slacked, and judgment doth never go forth: for the wicked doth compass about the righteous; therefore wrong judgment proceedeth.

Most of the prophets primarily declared God's message to people. In a sense, Habakkuk took Judah's cause before the Lord and sought answers to some hard questions.

The first question begins with words often asked about prayers that seem not to be answered or even heard: **how long**? Habakkuk's prayer was called a **cry** that God had **not** heard, or so it seemed to Habakkuk. He had prayed about **violence,** but God did not **save.** The prophet saw **iniquity** ("wrongdoing," NRSV) and **grievance** ("wickedness," NASB; "trouble," NRSV). The last part of verse 3 lists four results of sin that troubled the prophet: **spoiling** ("destruction," NIV, NASB) . . . **violence** . . . **strife** . . . **contention.** These words picture a lawless society.

Each line of verse 4 makes the sins more specific. In **the law is slacked, slacked** is a word meaning to be cold or numb. "The law is paralyzed" (NIV). The law of God gave much attention to ensuring justice, but the law was paralyzed into inaction. **Judgment** translates *mishpat,* a key Old Testament word meaning "justice" (NIV). Habakkuk's view of the state of justice in Judah was very negative. Although God had clearly decreed justice, "justice never prevails" (NIV). Instead of a just society, they had a corrupt, unjust society. The reason for this was that **the wicked doth compass about the righteous** ("the wicked hem in the righteous," NIV). The well-to-do members of society were often the most wicked and underhanded. Thus the rich often used their positions to overwhelm the righteous poor. **Therefore wrong judgment proceedeth** ("justice is perverted," NIV).

Habakkuk's questions were reverent prayers to God. God accepts sincere questions addressed to Him with reverence and trust. He condemns cynical questions spoken to other people. We see the difference in how God answered Habakkuk.

What are the lasting lessons in Habakkuk 1:2-4?

1. Sins of injustice and violence plague human society.
2. People of faith ask God for justice and peace.
3. At times this prayer seems to go unanswered.
4. People of faith sometimes ask God when this prayer will be answered.

God Is at Work (Hab. 1:5-6)

How did God answer Habakkuk's first set of questions? What new revelation did He give to Habakkuk? How did He describe the Chaldeans?

***1:5-6:* Behold ye among the heathen, and regard, and wonder marvelously: for I will work a work in your days, which ye will not believe, though it be told you. [6]For, lo, I raise up the Chaldeans, that bitter and hasty nation, which shall march through the breadth of the land, to possess the dwelling places that are not theirs.**

Habakkuk's first question was essentially the question nearly everyone asks at times. Why does God allow evil people to get by with mistreating good people? God responds to this question in a variety of ways. Seldom does He offer a careful and complete explanation of what He does or what He doesn't do. God accepted Habakkuk's words in verses 2-4 as a sincere prayer, so He revealed to the prophet a part of the answer to his concern about the injustice, sin, and violence of his own people. The answer, however, was not what Habakkuk expected or wanted.

The prophet had his attention on Judah. God told Habakkuk to **behold** what was going on in other lands. "Look among the nations! Observe! Be astonished! Wonder!" (NASB). God was at work in the world outside Judah. As Sovereign God, He moves in the affairs of nations and people to accomplish His purposes. God was doing something in the prophet's own lifetime that he would **not believe** even after being **told.**

I raise up the Chaldeans, that bitter and hasty nation ("I am raising up the Babylonians, that ruthless and impetuous people," NIV). **Chaldeans** is just another name for the Babylonians. The history of Israel is intertwined with that of other nations. At some points the secular history of ancient times intersected the history of the Israelites. The Israelites were delivered from slavery in Egypt, the super power of that time. Assyria destroyed the Northern Kingdom of Israel and threatened the Southern Kingdom of Judah. God delivered Judah from Assyria, but many of the people concluded from this that God would protect them from all foreign armies. Almost no one believed Judah could be swallowed up as Israel had been. But God revealed to Jeremiah and Habakkuk that Babylonia would defeat Judah. This was the moment of revelation for Habakkuk.

God told him that the Babylonians would **march through the breadth of the land, to possess the dwelling places that are not theirs.** In the context of Habakkuk's questions, the prophet understood that God intended to use the Babylonians to chastise His own sinful people. Read verses 7-10 for further descriptions of these fierce warriors and God's plan to use them to capture Judah.

These verses were God's initial answer to Habakkuk's prayers about God's slowness to punish the sins of Judah. He had been patient and longsuffering with the people of Judah, but the time of retribution was near.

We know that God is at work in our world and in our lives. He is at work to bring in His kingdom. Looking back on our lives, as people of faith we can see evidences of God's hand guiding us. We can see evidences of His hand in human history. We see that sinful and ungodly nations may flourish for a while, but eventually they pass into dust. Nations that claim to honor God are prone to forget God and face His judgment.

What are the lasting lessons of Habakkuk 1:5-6?

1. God is the Sovereign Lord of human history.

2. He moves in the lives of people and in the affairs of nations to accomplish His plan and to bring in His kingdom.

3. Even His people marvel at His work.

The Righteous Suffer (Hab. 1:12-13)

How does verse 12 show the way Habakkuk understood God's response to his questions in verses 2-4? What new questions did this lead the prophet to ask?

1:12-13: **Art thou not from everlasting, O LORD my God, mine Holy One? we shall not die. O LORD, thou hast ordained them for judgment; and, O mighty God, thou hast established them for correction. ¹³Thou art of purer eyes than to behold evil, and canst not look on iniquity: wherefore lookest thou upon them that deal treacherously, and holdest thy tongue when the wicked devoureth the man that is more righteous than he?**

Habakkuk realized that he was hearing the answer to his questions from the **God** who is **everlasting.** He addressed Him as **O LORD my God, mine Holy One.** The words **we shall not die** seem to be an expression of confidence that God's people would not be totally destroyed. The **mighty God** had **ordained them for judgment** and **established them for correction** ("chastisement," RSV). In other words, God was chastising and correcting His erring people. Verse 12 shows that Habakkuk understood what the Lord had said; however, verse 13 shows that the new revelation presented new problems for him. Verses 2-4 show Habakkuk's concern about sinful Jews running roughshod over fellow Jews. Verse 13 shows his concern that God would use a nation of ungodly people to chastise His own people.

Thou art of purer eyes than to behold evil, and canst not look on iniquity. Because God is holy, He cannot approve **evil** or **iniquity.** Everything about the holy God is opposed to sin. How then could He **look** upon **them that deal treacherously,** an obvious reference to the Babylonians? How could God use **the wicked** to devour **the man that is more righteous than he?** Some of the Israelites had sinned, but their sins paled by comparison to the evil of the Babylonians. Habakkuk was deeply disturbed by God's plan to use this heathen nation to overcome Judah. And true to his past practice, Habakkuk asked the Lord about this. The word translated **look** in the question means more than to gaze at something. It means to "look with approval." The second question in verse 13 assumed that God approved because God held His tongue: "Why are you silent while the wicked swallow up those more righteous than themselves" (NIV). Verses 14-17 expand on the cruelty and idolatry of these evil people.

What are the lasting lessons in Habakkuk 1:12-13?

1. Mature believers realize that God sometimes must correct His sinful people.

2. They sometimes have questions about how God chooses to chastise His own.

3. If such questions are asked sincerely and reverently, they are prayers.

Live by Faith (Hab. 2:2-4,18-20)

How did God respond to Habakkuk's second group of questions? How did the prophet exemplify the **faith** *of 2:4? How do verses 18-19 answer the prophet's questions? How does verse 20 represent a new level of the prophet's faith?*

2:2-4: And the LORD answered me, and said, Write the vision, and make it plain upon tables, that he may run that readeth it. ³For the vision is yet for an appointed time, but at the end it shall speak, and not lie: though it tarry, wait for it; because it will surely come, it will not tarry. ⁴Behold, his soul which is lifted up is not upright in him: but the just shall live by his faith.

Receiving no immediate answer to this new dilemma, Habakkuk resolved to wait for God to respond to his question and to prepare his own response to God's response (2:1). As Habakkuk waited, God told him, **Write the vision, and make it plain upon tables, that he may run that readeth it.** If this is the correct translation, it means that the message is important enough to be heralded abroad. This instruction may also be translated, "Write it clearly enough to be read at a glance" (CEV). The meaning would be that the writing would be so large that a passerby could read it.

The time of fulfillment of the vision was **yet for an appointed time.** That is, the time was still in the future; but it was sure to come because God appointed the time. Habakkuk was told, **Wait for it; because it will surely come, it will not tarry.**

Verse 4 contrasts two kinds of people. The person who is **lifted up is not upright in him.** People who are puffed up with pride and self-importance are not righteous in the sight of God. At this point the Lord was thinking of the arrogant Babylonians, but it would also apply to the proud in Judah. By contrast, **the just** ("righteous," NIV) **shall live by his faith.** Christians are familiar with the last part of verse 4 because Paul quoted it to teach justification by faith in Christ (Rom. 1:17; Gal. 3:11). Some Bible students believe that the word in verse 4 means "faithfulness." *Faith* and *faithfulness* are closely related. A person with real faith will be faithful.

2:18-20: What profiteth the graven image that the maker thereof hath graven it; the molten image, and a teacher of lies, that the maker of his work trusteth therein, to make dumb idols? [19]Woe unto him that saith to the wood, Awake; to the dumb stone, Arise, it shall teach! Behold, it is laid over with gold and silver, and there is no breath at all in the midst of it. [20]But the LORD is in his holy temple: let all the earth keep silence before him.

Habakkuk 2:6-20 pronounces five woes on the invading Babylonians. They would ride high for a while, but their sins would eventually bring them down. The Lord condemned them for greed and violence (vv. 6-8), a false sense of security (vv. 9-11), disregard for human life (vv. 12-14), corruption of one's neighbors (vv. 15-17), and idolatry (vv. 18-20). The Babylonians had many gods and had images for each one. They mocked the Jews for their invisible God for whom they had no images. The Jews in turn mocked the man-made gods of idol worshippers.

Idols are lifeless creations of idol makers. A person makes an idol of wood or metal. Then he worships it and trusts in it. He calls on his god of **wood** or **stone,** but nothing he can do will make the image come alive or be able to help. Jeremiah referred to idols as broken cisterns (Jer. 2:13). The people had rejected God, who was like a fountain of water, and they had trusted in idols, which were like cisterns with holes in them. When thirsty people turn to broken cisterns, they find none of the water they seek and need.

Verse 20 is a striking contrast between lifeless idols and the Lord of heaven and earth. **His holy temple,** as used here, is heaven and earth, not a building in one fixed location. The Lord had promised Israel that His presence would be in their temple, but He could not be confined to any building. The call of God to all people is, **Let all the earth keep silence before him.** We can apply this to the need for reverence before God when we worship, but the meaning is deeper and broader. Paul used this analogy of silence to teach that we have no legitimate excuses for our sins (Rom. 3:19). The silence also represents our sense of unworthiness in the presence of Almighty God.

God had shown patience toward Habakkuk and his questions. He had answered some of the questions, but He also reminded the prophet and his readers that silence is a proper response to the awesome God who reigns over all.

What are the lasting lessons in Habakkuk 2:2-4,18-20?

1. Patiently waiting for the fulfillment of God's promises is one aspect of faith.

2. The righteous are people of faith and faithfulness.

3. Those who don't worship God often trust in lifeless idols.

4. An awareness of the awesome God calls for silence.

Hope in God (Hab. 3:17-19a)

Why are these verses one of the high-water marks of the Old Testament? How does the prophet's attitude move beyond questions?

3:17-19a: Although the fig tree shall not blossom, neither shall fruit be in the vines; the labor of the olive shall fail, and the fields shall yield no meat ["food," NIV]; **the flock shall be cut off from the fold, and there shall be no herd in the stalls: [18]Yet I will rejoice in the LORD, I will joy in the God of my salvation. [19a]The LORD God is my strength, and he will make my feet like hinds' feet, and he will make me to walk upon mine high places.**

Habakkuk 3 is a prayer in response to earlier questions and answers. The prophet asked for God to be merciful with the people He had delivered from Egypt. But Habakkuk believed that hard times lay ahead. How did the prophet respond to this prospect of dark days before the time of divine deliverance? In his own way, he did what Jeremiah did. He preached judgment before the judgment was at the gate of the city. Then he preached hope based on God's promises. Habakkuk shows how one person clung to God as he faced the ordeal of passing through the worst of times.

Verse 17 is a detailed description of the worst that can befall those who depend on the land for survival. They depended on figs, grapes, and olives; but Habakkuk anticipated that all three would fail, along with other crops. Also he foresaw the destruction of sheep and other livestock. Verse 17 is only a long series of introductory clauses, each enumerating some aspect of disaster. Verse 18 is the main clause. In it Habakkuk stated how he would respond to the catalog of disasters. In the context of the book, this shows that the prophet expected total breakdown of food supplies when the Babylonians came. Verse 18 shows the prophet's amazing response to the worst that could happen—**although** the food supply is taken away, **yet I will rejoice in the LORD, I will joy in the God of my salvation.**

Habakkuk was confident he could not only endure but also even **rejoice in the LORD.** In verse 19 he stated the basis for his confident hope: **The LORD God is my strength.** Habakkuk realized that as long as the Lord was with him, he could face any trial and even find **joy** in it. The joy came from the Lord's presence and help. *Hind* is another word for a deer. Habakkuk trusted God to make him as sure-footed as a deer is on the rocky mountain heights. The **high places** may signify either places of potential danger or inner spiritual heights—or it could include both. Verses 17-19 need to be read aloud to feel the power and poetry of the message. Judging from these final words, Habakkuk intended that the words be put to music.

Verses 17-19 are a high point in Old Testament faith. Often people of that day felt that hard times were not occasions for joy. Habakkuk had begun with questions about violence and injustice in his own land. Now he had come full circle. All of his questions were not answered, nor were all of his doubts resolved; but he had found the answer is a faith-relation with the Lord. He expressed his hope in terms of joy in the Lord. Even as New Testament believers we marvel at such expressions of joy in hard times.

What are the lasting lessons in Habakkuk 3:17-19a?

1. Although the worst may come, believers can rejoice in the Lord.

2. Believers can do this because God's presence strengthens and uplifts them.

❖ *Spiritual Transformations*

Habakkuk asked God why He allowed injustice and violence in Judah. God told him that He was sending the Babylonians to punish Judah. The prophet then asked how God could use an evil nation to defeat His own people. God's responses challenged Habakkuk to exercise faith and faithfulness. Habakkuk testified that he would continue to rejoice in the Lord even when the worst came to pass.

What questions do you ask God? _____

How do you respond when God shows you an answer? _____

How do you respond when God does not answer? _____

Prayer of Commitment: Lord, help me have the kind of relation with You that can rejoice even in the worst situations. Amen.

Study Theme

Peter's Principles for Successful Living

What is *success*? A general definition would be that success is achieving your goals. Nearly everyone would agree on this; but when people begin to list their goals, sharp differences emerge. Many people's goals are focused on financial success. Wise people realize that real success must be focused on other than financial goals.

During this study theme we will look at "Peter's Principles for Successful Living." The study is based on Peter's experiences as a disciple and his teachings in 1 Peter. Each of the five lessons focuses on one of the biblical goals for true success. The first lesson, "Know Jesus," is based on some episodes in Peter's life from the Gospels of Matthew and John: his initial encounter with Jesus, his call, and his walking on the water. The opposite quality to knowing and depending on Jesus is self-sufficiency.

The second lesson, "Live Confidently," is based on 1 Peter 1:1-12. Peter's confident hope was based on his regeneration and on Jesus' resurrection. The opposite of true confidence is self-confidence. The third lesson, "Act Right," is based on Focal Verses from 1 Peter 1:13–2:12. Christians need to show the reality of their faith by how they live. The opposite quality is self-indulgence. The fourth lesson, "Be Humble," is based on Focal Verses from 1 Peter 2:13–3:19 and 5:5-7. Humility is a basic Christian virtue. The opposite quality is self-assertion. The fifth lesson, "Take Courage," is based on verses from 1 Peter 3:13–4:19. Christians must be faithful in times of persecution. The opposite quality is self-preservation.

This study theme is designed to help you:
- live in relationship with Jesus Christ (Aug. 1)
- live confidently as a Christian (Aug. 8)
- act in the ways God desires (Aug. 15)
- live humbly (Aug. 22)
- show faithfulness and courage in your allegiance to Christ (Aug. 29)

Week of August 1

KNOW JESUS

Background Passages: Matthew 4:18-20; 14:22-33; John 1:35-42
Focal Passages: Matthew 4:18-20; 14:25-33; John 1:40-42
Key Verses: Matthew 4:19-20

❖ *Significance of the Lesson*

• The *Theme* of this lesson is that successful living begins with a relationship with Jesus Christ.
• The *Life Question* this lesson addresses is, What does a personal relationship with Jesus involve?
• The *Biblical Truth* is that a personal relationship with Jesus Christ involves spiritual transformation, discipleship, and faith.
• The *Life Impact* is to help you live in relationship with Jesus Christ.

Definitions of Success

Success is defined and measured in different ways by modern society—education, career, possessions, and prestige. True success, however, is defined and measured by God's standards. In the biblical worldview, successful living begins with a personal relationship with Jesus Christ and involves spiritual transformation.

Identifying with Simon Peter

Most of this study theme is based on what Peter wrote in his First Epistle, but the first lesson is based on three incidents in Peter's life. The Bible tells us much about Peter's life. We know more about him than any other apostle. He is a favorite Bible personality because we see so much of his human frailties, imperfections, failures, and sins. The Bible presents all of its people just as they were. When Oliver Cromwell prepared to have his portrait painted, he told the artist: "I desire you would use all your skill to paint my picture truly like me, and not flatter me at all; but remark all these roughnesses, pimples, warts, and everything as you see me."[1] From this came our saying "warts and all." The Bible paints Simon Peter warts and all. We see him at his highest moments, as at Pentecost; we see him at his lowest moments, as when he denied Jesus; and we see him at many moments when he soared and stumbled in the same incident.

Word Study: *Follow*

The Greek word *akoloutheo* literally means to "come after." It often means to "accompany" or "go along with" someone. It is often used in the Gospels to describe following as a disciple. Jesus invited people, "Follow me" (Matt. 4:19). Some of the crowd followed Jesus in the sense of going where He went, but His disciples did more than accompany Him. They committed themselves to learn from Him and obey Him. This is what it means to be a follower of Jesus.

❖ *Search the Scriptures*

In Peter's first contact with Jesus, the Lord gave him a new name signifying the transformation of Simon. Later, Jesus called Simon and Andrew to follow Him and to become fishers of men. During a storm on the Sea of Galilee, Jesus came toward the frightened disciples by walking on the water. Simon asked to walk to Jesus on the water, which he did until he took his eyes off Jesus, began to sink, and cried out to Jesus for deliverance.

The three outline points answer the Life Question.

Be Changed by Jesus (John 1:40-42)

*How did Andrew come to know Jesus? What is the meaning of the word **first**? What is the significance of the new name Jesus gave Simon? Why does being changed by Jesus require conversion and growth in Christlikeness?*

John 1:40-42: One of the two which heard John speak, and followed him, was Andrew, Simon Peter's brother. [41]He first findeth his own brother Simon, and saith unto him, We have found the Messias, which is, being interpreted, the Christ. [42]And he brought him to Jesus. And when Jesus beheld him, he said, Thou art Simon the son of Jona: thou shalt be called Cephas, which is by interpretation, A stone.

By the time John wrote his Gospel, Simon Peter was much more widely known than his brother. Thus although **Andrew** was the one who followed Jesus first, John identified him as **Simon Peter's brother.** God used the testimony of the lesser-known brother to win Peter. Before that happened, God had used the testimony of **John** the Baptist to win Andrew. John the Baptist had attracted lots of attention from many people. He was questioned at length by the religious leaders about who he claimed to be. He denied being the Christ, claiming only to be the voice of one crying in the wilderness, as prophesied by Isaiah (Isa. 40:3). Then when Jesus came to John, John loudly declared Jesus to be "the Lamb of God, which taketh away the sin of the world" (John 1:29).

John the Baptist had disciples of his own. He was standing with two of his disciples when Jesus walked nearby. John, who had publicly pointed to Jesus, privately did the same thing for these two disciples. Again he said, "Behold the Lamb of God" (v. 36). As a result, the two disciples of John followed Jesus. Verse 40 identifies Andrew as **one of the two which heard John speak, and followed** Jesus. The other one is unidentified but has been assumed to have been John the brother of James and the author of this Gospel.

The word **first** can be understood in three possible ways. Many people assume that the meaning is, "The first thing that Andrew did was to find his brother and tell him" (CEV). A second possibility is that the meaning is, "The first one Andrew told was his brother." The implication then would be that he also told others. A third possible meaning is, "He was the first to tell his brother," which implies that John also told his brother the same thing Andrew told Simon. Even though we do not know the exact meaning, very likely all three were true.

Some Bible students believe the form of the word translated **brought** implies some reluctance on the part of Simon, but that may be trying to read too much between the lines. We also know that Simon was not the only person whom Andrew brought to Jesus. Andrew seems to have been known as one who led others to Jesus. He was the disciple who brought to Jesus the boy whose lunch Jesus transformed so that over 5,000 could be fed (6:8-9). He was also the one who brought some Greeks who wanted to see Jesus (12:20-22). Andrew may not have been as gifted as his brother Peter; but if you or I could do only one thing, what better thing than the ability to introduce individuals to Jesus?

The word **found** is prominent in John's account of how the first of the twelve found Jesus. Our English word *eureka* is a transliteration of this word. This is what Archimedes said when he discovered a method for refining gold. It means, "I have found." The word occurs twice in verse 41, once in verse 43, and twice in verse 45. Andrew found his brother and told him, **We have found the Messias.** Because John's readers included many Gentiles, who were unfamiliar with Hebrew, John explained that **Messias** means the same as **Christ** ("the anointed one").

The word translated **beheld** refers to a concentrated, intense look. Jesus' eyes looked into the heart of the fisherman. Based on what He saw, Jesus gave Simon a new name, **Cephas,** the Aramaic word for **stone.** *Peter* comes from the Greek form of the word for rock. In ancient times names were significant because they represented the kind of person one was. Leon Morris explained: "The giving of a new name when done by men is an assertion of the authority of the giver (*e.g.* II Kings 23:34; 24:17). When done by God it speaks of a new character in which the man henceforth appears (*e.g.* Gen. 32:28). There is something of both ideas here. Simon is from this time Jesus' man. But he is also a different man, and the new name points to his character as 'the rock man.' Peter appears in all the Gospels as anything but a rock. He is impulsive, volatile, unreliable. But that was not God's last word for Peter. Jesus' words point to the change that would be wrought in him by the power of God."[2]

This was Peter's first encounter with Jesus. We aren't told what he said at the time, but later events show that he accepted his brother's testimony as true and thus he also believed. Peter's experience constituted a conversion. After he came to know Jesus, Peter was never again the same. Although Jesus is no longer here in the flesh, saving faith still involves a personal knowledge of Him. Through a growing knowledge of Christ, a person's life is transformed more and more into the image of Christ. The last recorded words of Peter were, "Grow in grace, and in the knowledge of our Lord and Savior Jesus Christ. To him be glory both now and forever. Amen" (2 Pet. 3:18).

The surest proof of a personal relation with Christ is a transformed life. According to the International Mission Board of the Southern Baptist Convention, believers worldwide prayed for a Christian prison inmate in Brazil who was badly beaten and threatened with death. An inmate who was a member of a Satanist group came to him, asking how to be saved. The inmate told the Christian he had been watching him ever since he became a believer. "You've changed so much since that time," he said. "Even when you were badly beaten, you didn't complain, and when you came back into the general life of the prison again, you just went on testifying what Jesus is doing for you." When the Christian shared God's plan of salvation with the Satanist, he accepted Jesus as Lord and began discipleship studies of his own.

What are the lasting lessons in John 1:40-42?

1. Saving faith is personal knowledge of Jesus Christ.

2. Believers should tell others about Jesus, beginning with their own families.

3. Being changed by Jesus begins with conversion and continues as we grow in Christ.

Follow Jesus (Matt. 4:18-20)

How does the call of Peter in Matthew 4:18-20 relate to John 1: 40-42 and Luke 5:1-11? How was the call of the twelve different from and how was it similar to the call to others to be disciples?

Matthew 4:18-20: And Jesus, walking by the sea of Galilee, saw two brethren, Simon called Peter, and Andrew his brother, casting a net into the sea: for they were fishers. [19]And he saith unto them, Follow me, and I will make you fishers of men. [20]And they straightway left their nets, and followed him.

This is the first encounter of Peter with Jesus that is told in the Gospel of Matthew. The invitation of **Jesus** and the responses of **Peter** and **Andrew** make more sense if we assume the earlier encounter in John 1:40-42. That is, the two fishermen already were believers in Jesus before the day He called them to be disciples.

The brothers were fishermen in **the sea of Galilee.** They were commercial fishermen who earned their living by selling their catch. Fish was one of the main foods of people in the region. The brothers were partners with another set of brothers, James and John (Luke 5:10). They fished using nets, which they cast from their boats or from the shore as they were doing when Jesus came **walking** along the shore. James and John were mending their nets (Matt. 4:21).

Jesus issued an invitation. The basic challenge was **Follow me.** This was an invitation to go with Jesus and accompany Him, but it was much more than this. Religious teachers gathered about them a group of close pupils and companions. The two fishermen realized Jesus was inviting them to be this kind of follower. These two and their partners became the nucleus of the twelve disciples, whose names are listed in 10:2-4. These twelve were special disciples. They spent time with Jesus, heard His teachings, witnessed His miracles. After His resurrection, Jesus appointed them to preserve and proclaim the message of the gospel of His death and resurrection and the things He said and did.

Jesus promised that He would **make** them **fishers of men.** They knew how to catch fish. Jesus taught them how to catch people for the kingdom of God. Luke 5:1-11 gives an expanded account of the events of that momentous day in Peter's life. The four fishermen had spent a disappointing night in which they had caught nothing. Jesus told them to go back out into deep water and cast their nets once more. Peter reluctantly obeyed, and they pulled in so many fish that the other boat had to come and help. The experience convicted Peter of his sinfulness, and he said to Jesus, "Depart from me; for I am a sinful man, O Lord" (v. 8). Rather than leaving, Jesus said, "Fear not; from hence-forth thou shalt catch men" (v. 10).

Peter was not always a good example for later followers, but the quickness of his initial response is how all people should respond to Jesus' call: **Follow me.** Peter and Andrew **straightway** ("immediately," HCSB; "at once," NIV) **left their nets, and followed him.** This stands in contrast to the way many people delay because they claim they have something else they must do first (see Luke 9:59-62).

The word *disciples* is one of the names by which followers of Jesus are known. Peter and the rest of the twelve were unique disciples in some ways, but in other ways they were examples of what all disciples should be. Three characteristics of theirs fit all of us who follow Jesus. First, they were with Jesus. They were with Him in the flesh during His earthly ministry, and after Pentecost they knew Him in Spirit—the way all later disciples know Him. We need to live a life of prayer and we need to practice Jesus' presence. Second, disciples are students of the Lord. He invites people to learn of Him and to learn from Him. Because of our personal relationship with Him this role of disciples involves becoming more like Jesus. The third characteristic of all disciples is to go forth in Jesus' name. His mission is our mission. He wants to work in and through us to win the lost and to serve others in His name.

Some people think of discipleship as an optional feature separate from salvation. Yet Jesus taught that anyone who wants to follow Him must be totally committed to Him and to His way of the cross.

What are the lasting lessons in Matthew 4:18-20?
1. The call to follow Jesus is a call to become a disciple.
2. This call comes to all Christians.
3. Our response to Jesus' call should be immediate and total.

Trust Jesus (Matt. 14:25-33)

Why were the disciples crossing the water without Jesus? How did Jesus respond to their fear when they saw Him walking on the water? Why did Peter ask to come to Jesus? Why did he begin to sink? How was this incident typical of Peter's relation to Jesus? What was the final response of the disciples to what happened?

Matthew 14:25-27: And in the fourth watch of the night Jesus went unto them, walking on the sea. ²⁶And when the disciples saw him walking on the sea, they were troubled, saying, It is a spirit; and they cried out for fear. ²⁷But straightway Jesus spake unto them, saying, Be of good cheer; it is I; be not afraid.

The background to this incident was what happened after Jesus fed the 5,000 (vv. 15-21). Verse 22 says that Jesus "constrained ("made," HCSB) his disciples to get into a ship, and to go before him unto the other side, while he sent the multitudes away." Then Jesus went to a mountain alone to pray (v. 23). Why did Jesus have to force His disciples into a boat and send them across the sea? The answer is in the parallel passage in John 6:15. After Jesus fed the multitude, the people tried to force Jesus to be their king. The feeding of so many hungry people convinced many that Jesus was the kind of Messiah for whom they had been waiting—one who would feed the hungry and defeat their enemies. Apparently His disciples were in the middle of this movement, or they were at least sympathetic with it. So Jesus got them into a boat and headed them away from the place.

For Jesus, this was a renewal of the temptations to use His power to achieve what the people wanted, not what God knew they needed. So Jesus withdrew to be alone with His Father. However, while He was not with the disciples, a storm swept down on the Sea of Galilee. Sudden fierce storms are frequent on that body of water. The boat was far from land, the waves were high, and the wind was against them. We can easily imagine their feelings. In an earlier storm, the disciples were terrified even when Jesus was with them in the boat (Matt. 8:23-25). Now they were in a deadly storm, and Jesus was not with them—or so they thought. Life has its storms. Sometimes we feel not only frightened but also alone. We think that we are alone and that the Lord either doesn't know or doesn't care.

Hours had passed since they left. It was **in the fourth watch of the night.** The Romans divided the 12 hours from 6 p.m. to 6 a.m. into four watches of three hours each. Therefore it was between 3 and 6 a.m., probably "around three in the morning" (HCSB). At that point they saw a figure that looked like Jesus, but the figure was not in their boat or in any other boat. The figure was **walking on the sea.** Rather than being reassured, **they were troubled** ("terrified," NIV, HCSB). **It is a spirit** ("ghost," NIV, HCSB). The disciples **cried out for fear.** Even when the Lord comes to our aid in life's storms, we sometimes fail to recognize Him, and thus His coming only increases our fears.

Then Jesus spoke and revealed three things. He called on them to **Be of good cheer** ("Have courage!" HCSB). He assured them that He was no ghostly apparition, stating, **It is I.** Then He said, **Be not afraid.** In the Bible, God, an angel, or Jesus often spoke these words! Fear paralyzes us and makes us vulnerable to even worse responses.

Matthew 14:28-33: **And Peter answered him and said, Lord, if it be thou, bid me come unto thee on the water. [29]And he said, Come. And when Peter was come down out of the ship, he walked on the water, to go to Jesus. [30]But when he saw the wind boisterous, he was afraid; and beginning to sink, he cried, saying, Lord, save me. [31]And immediately Jesus stretched forth his hand, and caught him, and said unto him, O thou of little faith, wherefore didst thou doubt? [32]And when they were come into the ship, the wind ceased. [33]Then they that were in the ship came and worshiped him, saying, Of a truth thou art the Son of God.**

At this point Peter spoke up. He probably had to shout in order to be heard above the sound of the storm. The word **if** may reflect some lingering vestige of uncertainty, but whatever fears and doubts he felt, Peter said, **Bid me come unto thee on the water.** We aren't told why Peter made this request. We do know that he often took the lead among the apostles. We also know Peter was impulsive. His request showed courage and faith.

Jesus said to the disciple, **Come.** Peter then got **down out of the ship** and **walked on the water, to go to Jesus.** The Bible doesn't tell how far Jesus was from the ship, nor does it say how far Peter walked, but it does say that for a while Peter **walked on the water.** This, of course, was a miracle just as it was for Jesus to walk on the water.

As long as Peter kept his eyes fixed on Jesus, he was upheld from sinking into the sea. But when Peter took his eyes off Jesus and **saw the wind boisterous,** everything changed. The howling wind and the high waves reminded Peter that a human being couldn't walk on water. At this point, **he was afraid; and** he was **beginning to sink.** By looking from Jesus to the storm, fear replaced faith.

However, Peter still had enough faith to cry out, **Lord, save me.** Jesus acted **immediately.** He **stretched forth his hand, and caught him.** Although Jesus called Peter a person **of little faith** and chided him for his **doubt,** Jesus did not reject Simon as an unbelieving doubter. He realized that Peter had shown courage and faith in asking to walk on the sea and actually leaving the boat and walking toward Jesus. Peter's problem came when he focused on the storm and took his eyes off Jesus. Jesus' rescue of Peter shows that He saw Peter's cry for help as an expression of one who believed in Jesus' power to save. Peter's faith faltered, but he at least made the venture. And he called to the Lord for help. There is a big difference between the doubts of a real un-believer and the faltering faith of a real believer. Doubt is the normal stance of an unbeliever; faith is the normal stance of a believer. But the faith of believers is seldom perfect. Sometimes we falter; but although the Lord rebukes us for our imperfect faith, He does not let us sink.

Jesus came to the boat holding Peter firmly in His grasp—**and when they were come into the ship, the wind ceased.** The other disciples had witnessed all of this. They realized that Jesus was much more than the Messiah. They **worshiped him** and declared Him to be **the Son of God.**

Translations of the Bible into English use several words to describe how people ought to respond to the Lord. The three most common are *belief, faith,* and *trust.* Each of these is a good word and can be used to describe our response to the Lord. But *trust* has many characteristics of the biblical ideal of a personal relationship with the Lord. It has the advantage of being a word used in healthy human relations. It strongly implies not only faith in the Lord's power but also confidence in His love and care.

> Simply trusting ev'ry day,
> Trusting thro' a stormy way;
> Even when my faith is small,
> Trusting Jesus, that is all.[3]

What are the lasting lessons in Matthew 14:25-33?
1. People of faith sometimes find themselves in one of life's storms.
2. Our initial response may be to wonder where the Lord is.
3. Jesus knows and cares about us.
4. He comes to us in His own time and way.
5. He calls for faith and courage instead of doubt and fear.
6. Our response often is a mixture of faith and doubt.
7. Jesus helps us when we cry out to Him.

❖ *Spiritual Transformations*

When Simon (Peter) first met Jesus, the Lord gave him the name Cephas (rock), which signified the transformation Jesus brought to Simon's life. Jesus called Peter and Andrew to follow Him as disciples, and they immediately left all to follow Him. Jesus came walking on the water when a storm caught the disciples on the Sea of Galilee. Peter asked to be allowed to walk on the water to Jesus; but after beginning, he looked away from Jesus to the storm and began to sink. When he cried out to Jesus, the Lord grasped his hand and saved him.

Simon Peter had a personal relationship with Jesus. He not only knew Jesus during His earthly ministry, but he also continued to grow in the personal knowledge of Jesus. Three marks of knowing Jesus are being personally transformed, following Him as a disciple, and trusting Him amidst the storms of life.

How have you become more like Jesus since you first came to know Him? _____

What kind of a follower of Jesus are you? _____

How do you trust Jesus during life's storms? _____

Prayer of Commitment: Lord, enrich the personal relationship I have with You. Amen.

[1]Cited in John Bartlett, *Familiar Quotations*, 15th edition [Boston: Little, Brown and Company, 1980], 272.

[2]Leon Morris, *The Gospel According to John*, in The New International Commentary on the New Testament [Grand Rapids: William B. Eerdmans Publishing Company, 1971], 160-161.

[3]Edgar Page Stites, "Trusting Jesus," No. 417, *The Baptist Hymnal*, 1991.

LIVE CONFIDENTLY

Bible Passage: 1 Peter 1:1-12
Key Verses: 1 Peter 1:8-9

❖ *Significance of the Lesson*

• The *Theme* of this lesson is that successful living includes living confidently in the resources God provides.
• The *Life Question* this lesson addresses is, What factors enable me to live with more confidence as a Christian?
• The *Biblical Truth* is that God makes His resources available to believers so they can live confidently even in the midst of trials.
• The *Life Impact* is to help you live confidently as a Christian.

Confident Living in Chaotic Times

World crises and personal troubles cause many people to live in fear and uncertainty. Christians are not immune to such feelings when faced with difficulties beyond their control. While some people put their confidence in resources of their own, Christians are able to live with confident hope based on the resources and promises of God.

Word Study: *Heaviness*

The active form of the Greek word *lupeo* means "to grieve," "to irritate," or "to vex" (see Eph. 4:30). The passive form, which appears in 1 Peter 1:6, means "to be distressed" (HCSB). The *King James Version* has "in heaviness." The related noun *lupe* means "grief," "sorrow," or "pain" (see John 16:21).

❖ *Search the Scriptures*

Peter wrote to Christians in several Roman provinces of Asia Minor. He emphasized the initiative God took in making them His people in a lost world. He praised God for endowing these children of His with living hope based on Christ's resurrection. This hope is an inheritance kept for believers. Although they were passing through fiery trials, they could rejoice. The prophets had foretold this good news.

The Divine Initiative (1 Pet. 1:1-2)

What do these verses reveal about the geographical location of the recipients of the letter? What do they reveal about their spiritual condition?

Verses 1-2: Peter, an apostle of Jesus Christ, to the strangers scattered throughout Pontus, Galatia, Cappadocia, Asia, and Bithynia, ²elect according to the foreknowledge of God the Father, through sanctification of the Spirit, unto obedience and sprinkling of the blood of Jesus Christ: Grace unto you, and peace, be multiplied.

Our letters today begin with the name of the one to whom the letter is sent. We reveal the writer's name at the end. Letters written in the first century began with the name of the letter writer. **Peter** was well-known among Christians. He was **an apostle,** he had been with Jesus from the beginning of His ministry, was a witness of the resurrection, and was appointed by Jesus (see Acts 1:21-26).

Peter wrote to **strangers scattered throughout Pontus, Galatia, Cappadocia** [kap-uh-DOH-shih-uh], **Asia, and Bithynia** [bih-THIN-ih-uh]. The three middle names were provinces in northern Asia Minor. The first and last names were two regions in the same province. This area is now modern-day Turkey.

Peter described the recipients with words that are elsewhere used of Jewish people. The English word **strangers** refers to people with whom we are not acquainted. Here it translates *parepidemois,* which was used of people away from home in a foreign land. It is translated in various ways: "temporary residents," (HCSB), "exiles," (NRSV), "aliens," (NASB). It is translated "pilgrims" in Hebrews 11:13, because believers' true citizenship is in heaven (Heb. 11:10; Phil. 3:20). **Scattered** is the Greek word *diaspora,* which sometimes is called the "Dispersion" (NRSV, HCSB). This word became a technical term for Jews who lived outside the promised land.

Elect is *eklektos,* which means "chosen," and is often used of Jews as God's chosen people. In the New Testament it refers to the reality that our relation with God is based on His love. Believers are **elect according to the foreknowledge of God the Father.** Trace your salvation back to its source, and that route will lead you back to the loving heart of the eternal God. He knew us and sought us long before we came to know Him.

Peter said believers were chosen by **God the Father, through sanctification of the Spirit.** As sinners are declared righteous through faith, believers are sanctified or set apart for holy living through the work of the Spirit.

Obedience and **sprinkling of the blood** are familiar Old Testament terms. When God offered His covenant to Israel, He demanded that they obey (Ex. 19:5). The covenant was sealed by sprinkling the blood of animals on the people (24:1-8). The new covenant is sealed by the shed **blood of Jesus Christ** (see 1 Pet. 1:18-19).

"We have therefore the three steps taken by the three persons of the Triune God. God the Father chooses the sinner to salvation. God the Spirit brings the sinner thus chosen to the act of faith. God the Son cleanses him in His precious blood."[1]

What are the lasting lessons in 1 Peter 1:1-2?

1. Christians are pilgrims on earth whose true citizenship is in heaven.

2. When believers trace their salvation to its source, it leads to the loving heart of the eternal God, our Heavenly Father.

3. The Spirit sets believers apart for holy living.

4. The blood of Christ cleanses believers and calls them to obedient living.

The Living Hope (1 Pet. 1:3-5)

Why is praise the basic language of faith? In what ways do these verses enable Christians to live with confidence?

Verses 3-5: Blessed be the God and Father of our Lord Jesus Christ, which according to his abundant mercy hath begotten us again unto a lively hope by the resurrection of Jesus Christ from the dead, ⁴to an inheritance incorruptible, and undefiled, and that fadeth not away, reserved in heaven for you, ⁵who are kept by the power of God through faith unto salvation ready to be revealed in the last time.

The opening words **blessed be** preceding God's name were often used by the Jews (Gen. 9:26; Ps. 66:20). Peter used it with the Christian name for God—**the God and Father of our Lord Jesus Christ.** Peter praised God before writing about Him. The basic language of faith is addressed *to* God, not *about* Him. And the first thing to say to God is to praise Him. Peter praised God for **his abundant mercy,** noting God has **begotten us again.** The terminology is not exactly the same as what Jesus said to Nicodemus about being born anew or again, but the teaching is the same. God gives believers new life. This is more than a second chance to do better. It is a new source and kind of life.

Believers are born again **unto a lively** ("living," NIV, HCSB) **hope.** The Greek word for hope is *elpis.* The biblical notion of hope has two components: desire and expectation. In the vocabulary of faith, a third element is added—confidence. This confidence does not mean that the everyday hopes of Christians are sure to happen. True confidence is limited to the promises of God. The Greeks had many hopes and dreams, but apart from God, they had no real hope. Paul wrote, "At that time ye were without Christ, being aliens from the common-wealth of Israel, and strangers from the covenants of promise, having no hope, and without God in the world" (Eph. 2:12). People are hungry for hope, and what they need is a living hope. The basis for living hope is **the resurrection of Jesus Christ from the dead.** Some people have all kinds of hopes in life based on something other than Jesus Christ's victory over death. Christ's resurrection is the most solid foundation for confidence.

The content of the living hope is **an inheritance.** As God's children, we are heirs. Peter used three words to describe our inheritance. Each word begins with the first letter of the Greek alphabet, *alpha.* This letter before a word often means what the English prefix *un* means; that is, the letter makes the word mean the opposite of what it would mean otherwise. *Aphthartos* means **incorruptible** ("imperishable," HCSB). *Amiantos* means **undefiled** ("uncorrupted," HCSB). *Amarantos* means **fadeth not away** ("unfading," HCSB). This "inheritance . . . can never perish, spoil or fade" (NIV). This inheritance contrasts with earthly inheritances that for many reasons are far from certain. The giver of this inheritance is the eternal God who owns all things and always keeps His word.

Another reason for confidence is that the inheritance is **reserved in heaven for you.** Not only is the inheritance reserved but also each believer is **kept by the power of God. Kept** translates *phroureo,* which was used to describe being under military protection or guard. Christians "are being protected by God's power" (HCSB; "shielded by God's power," NIV). All of these facts build confidence in God and His promises: The inheritance is reserved, and we are protected by God's power. Nothing could be more sure.

The goal of the living hope is **salvation ready to be revealed in the last time.** We often speak of salvation in the past tense. Christians have been saved from the penalty of sin. This is called justification or regeneration. But we are also still in the process of being saved from the power of sin. This is called sanctification. Peter was referring to the future consummation of salvation from the presence of sin. This is glorification. No one skips the earlier stages and receives the final stage. On the positive side, all who experience the earlier stages can be sure of the final stage. This is because each stage is based on God's grace and power. As Paul wrote in Philippians 1:6, "I am sure of this, that He who started a good work in you will carry it on to completion until the day of Christ Jesus" (HCSB).

What are the lasting lessons in 1 Peter 1:3-5?

1. The basic language of faith is praise to God.

2. Because of God's mercy, believers have been born again as God's children.

3. Christians have a living hope.

4. Our hope is based on the resurrection of Jesus Christ from the dead.

5. The content of our hope is the inheritance reserved for those who are guarded by the power of God.

6. The goal of hope is the final stage of the salvation begun in this life.

The Inexpressible Joy (1 Pet. 1:6-9)

How can Christians rejoice in times of grief and trials? Why is the trying of faith more precious than gold? How can people believe what they cannot see? Why is joy inexpressible?

Verses 6-9: **Wherein ye greatly rejoice, though now for a season, if need be, ye are in heaviness through manifold temptations: [7]that the trial of your faith, being much more precious than of gold that perisheth, though it be tried with fire, might be found unto praise and honor and glory at the appearing of Jesus Christ: [8]whom having not seen, ye love; in whom, though now ye see him not, yet believing, ye rejoice with joy unspeakable and full of glory: [9]receiving the end of your faith, even the salvation of your souls.**

Two themes run through these verses—trials and joy. These two themes seem to be mutually exclusive. By secular standards, no sane person would rejoice in the midst of real troubles. Yet the Bible teaches that people of faith rejoice in the worst of times.

The last part of verse 6 describes the trials as **manifold temptations. Heaviness** can be translated "distressed" (HCSB) or "suffer grief" (NIV). **Temptations** translates *peirasmos,* which means a test. It can refer to a *temptation* to do evil or to a *trial* allowed by God for good. Only the context of a passage can determine which English word is better to use. Most translators think Peter was referring to "trials" (NIV, HCSB). Peter no doubt was thinking of the persecution his readers were experiencing. **For a season** ("for a short time," HCSB; "for a little while," NIV) is true of all earthly trials when compared to eternity. Even if the trials last till death, Paul wrote, "I reckon that the sufferings of this present time are not worthy to be compared with the glory which shall be revealed in us" (Rom. 8:18).

Peter told his readers they could **greatly rejoice** in their trials because God can bring good out of faithfulness in such times. The word **trial** in verse 7 is not the same word as **temptations** in verse 6. The word in verse 7 is *dokimion,* which refers to something that has been tested and "proved genuine" (NIV). Such **faith** is **much more precious than of gold that perisheth, though it be tried with fire.** "Just as men use fire to distinguish gold from counterfeit, so God uses trials to distinguish genuine faith from superficial profession. *Gold* is here used in comparison because, although it is only part of this perishable creation, it is of sufficient value, compared with other things with which it may be mixed and confused, to have its genuineness discovered and demonstrated by the test of fire. Since *faith* is in God's sight faith so much more precious, and has, when genuine, imperishable value, it is understandable that God should similarly use the fires of trial to discover and to demonstrate where true faith exists. So the trials of our earthly experience are not to be regarded as strange or surprising, but as providentially ordered for divine and eternal ends (cf. 4:10)."[2]

God's long-range goal is that such genuine faith **might be found unto praise and honor and glory at the appearing of Jesus Christ.** Peter made sure that the focus not be turned on believers and our inheritance but on the Lord who is coming to complete His saving work. He is the One to receive **praise and honor and glory.** As an apostle, Peter had actually seen Jesus; but he knew his readers had never seen the Lord. Yet they responded to Christ with **love.** He wrote of them, "And though not seeing Him now, you believe in Him and rejoice with inexpressible and glorious joy" (1 Pet. 1:8, HCSB).

Verse 9 returns to the theme at the end of verse 5, the future stage of salvation. The **end** ("goal," NIV, HCSB) **of** their **faith** would be **the salvation of** their **souls.**

Thus rather than our confidence being shaken by trials, we can see trials as opportunities for confidence building as they highlight the genuineness and eternal quality of our faith.

What are the lasting lessons of 1 Peter 1:6-9?

1. Christians can rejoice in times of trials.
2. Trials test faith and prove whether it is genuine.
3. Genuine faith glorifies Christ.
4. Joy in troubles should build confidence, not destroy it.

The Revealed Gospel (1 Pet. 1:10-12)

What role did the prophets play in the revealed gospel? How did they foresee future events? How did the message of the prophets reach Peter's readers? Why did angels desire to look into the gospel?

Verses 10-12: **Of which salvation the prophets have inquired and searched diligently, who prophesied of the grace that should come unto you: [11]searching what, or what manner of time the Spirit of Christ which was in them did signify, when it testified beforehand the sufferings of Christ, and the glory that should follow. [12]Unto whom it was revealed, that not unto themselves, but unto us they did minister the things, which are now reported unto you by them that have preached the gospel unto you with the Holy Ghost** [Spirit] **sent down from heaven; which things the angels desire to look into.**

The word **salvation** appears for the third time in Peter's opening words (vv. 5,9,10). He emphasized the crucial work of **the prophets** in this salvation. Although there were prophets in the New Testament, Peter had in mind the prophets of Old Testament times. Although much of what the prophets said was directed toward people of their day, Peter was interested in their predictions concerning the future. They **inquired and searched diligently** concerning **salvation.** They **prophesied of the grace that should come unto you.** They were seeking to discern the time and circumstances that would be revealed to them concerning **the sufferings of Christ, and the glory that should follow.** Throughout Jesus' ministry, He tried to tell His disciples of the necessity of His sufferings, death, and resurrection. After Jesus' resurrection, He opened the Scriptures and showed them how the Scriptures foretold all this (Luke 24:44-46).

How were the prophets able to predict these events? They spoke as they were carried along by the Spirit (2 Pet. 1:21). The Holy Spirit is called **the Spirit of Christ** in verse 11. This Spirit **was in them.** He guided as they searched the future and **testified beforehand** of Christ's death and resurrection. As we read the sermon Peter preached at Pentecost, we see some of these prophecies (Acts 2: 14-36). Philip was able to witness and win the Ethiopian, who was reading the most famous prophecy of Christ's sufferings in bearing the sins of humanity—Isaiah 53 (see Acts 8:26-40).

The inspired words of the prophets were in the Scriptures from which the early preachers declared the good news. The believers to whom Peter wrote had heard the good news from such preachers. The prophets did not live to see the fulfillment of their prophecies, but they wrote not for **themselves** but for those who would hear the good news of which they wrote.

Peter closed verse 12 with a tantalizing reference to **angels.** Referring to the good news of salvation, Peter wrote, **which things the angels desire to look into.** How we are to understand these words depends on how we view the word **desire.** Is the desire fulfilled or unfulfilled? If the desire has been fulfilled, the meaning is that the angels have a continuing interest in the salvation of sinful humanity. If the desire is unfulfilled, the meaning is that the angels have not experienced the kind of salvation from sin that saved humans have experienced; therefore, angels have an intense interest, even curiosity, in wanting to look into what is involved in God's great plan of salvation. We know that angels such as Gabriel were involved in revealing God's plan. But while angels have been involved in what God has done and is doing, angels have not experienced saving grace for sinners.

What are the lasting lessons in 1 Peter 1:10-12?

1. The Old Testament prophets were led by the Spirit to predict the suffering and glory of Jesus Christ.

2. Their prophecies were revealed by the risen Lord to the apostles, and these facts became the good news by which people are saved when they respond to the message of salvation.

3. The angels have an intense interest in God's great salvation of sinful humans.

❖ *Spiritual Transformations*

Peter addressed his readers as pilgrims of faith whom God chose by His initiative. He praised the Lord for the living hope based on the resurrection of Jesus Christ from the dead. The hope was an inheritance reserved for those being saved. Although they were experiencing trials, they could rejoice as they confidently awaited Christ's appearing. They had believed the gospel prophesied by Spirit-inspired prophets, fulfilled in Christ, and preached to them.

Are you living with confidence? Usually the word *confidence* is used with the word *self*. People often speak of *self-confidence.* They usually mean by this a person whose confidence is based on his or her ability to rely on personal abilities to do things without fear of failure. Confidence for Christians, however, is based on knowing the Lord and relying on Him.

On December 30, 2002 three missionaries in Jibla, Yemen, were beginning a new day of service in the hospital. Martha Myers was a physician. William Koehn was the hospital administrator. Kathy Gariety was the purchasing agent. Without warning, an armed man burst into their morning meeting, and the gunman killed the three missionaries. One of their coworkers said that if the gunman intended to take their lives, he failed. "This [gunman] did not take their lives; they chose to give their lives long ago when they responded to God's call," said John Brady, who leads International Mission Board work in Northern Africa and the Middle East. These missionaries lived and died with confidence because they were where God wanted them to be and doing what He called them to do. The gunman ended their lives on earth, but as Christians they had a living hope based on the resurrection of Jesus. This gave them confidence to do their work and to leave their lives in the Lord's hands.

Are you living with the kind of confidence with which these three missionaries lived and died? _____

What part of 1 Peter 1:1-12 speaks most personally to you at this time in your life? _____

Prayer of Commitment: Blessed be the God and Father of our Lord Jesus Christ for the confidence He provides. Amen.

[1]Kenneth S. Wuest, *First Peter in the Greek New Testament,* in *Wuest's Word Studies in the Greek New Testament,* vol. 2 [Grand Rapids: William B. Eerdmans Publishing Company, 1942], 17.

[2]Alan M. Stibbs, *The First Epistle General of Peter,* in The Tyndale New Testament Commentaries [Grand Rapids: William B. Eerdmans Publishing Company, 1960], 78.

ACT RIGHT

Background Passage: 1 Peter 1:13–2:12
Focal Passages: 1 Peter 1:13-16,22-25; 2:1-3,11-12
Key Verse: 1 Peter 1:15

❖ *Significance of the Lesson*

• The *Theme* of this lesson is that successful living includes living in holiness.
• The *Life Question* this lesson addresses is, How should I act as a Christian?
• The *Biblical Truth* is that the Christian life is to be marked by holiness, love, maturity, and honor.
• The *Life Impact* is to help you act in the ways God desires.

Consistent Christian Behavior

Non-Christians expect Christians to live consistent Christian lives. When believers do not practice what they profess, they lose not only the joy of their salvation but also credibility in other people's eyes. Everyone deplores hypocrisy. Genuine Christians realize that right beliefs are important and that right behavior goes with right beliefs.

Word Study: *Holy*

The Greek word *hagios* and its Hebrew counterpart originally referred to anything set apart. God is holy because He is set apart from all things, since He is the Creator of all things. The word also refers to God's character as righteous and pure. In the same way, the basic idea in being holy people is that they are set apart by God and for God. Along with this came the moral holiness required for those set apart by and for the holy God (Lev. 11:44; 1 Pet. 1:15-16). The English word *holy* is kin to another set of English words used to translate *hagios* and its related words: "sanctify" *(hagiazo)* and "holiness" and "sanctification" *(hagiasmos)*. The plural of *hagios* is often translated "saints."

❖ Search the Scriptures

Believing in the Lord's future coming motivates alertness and sober living. Christians are to avoid conforming to the sins of their pre-Christian lives. They are to be holy as God is holy. Those who obey the truth practice love for one another. They are born again by the word of God. Christians put aside sins and grow like newborn babies as they feed on God's Word. They are strangers and pilgrims passing through this sinful world. Christians should silence the slanders against them by doing right.

Be Holy (1 Pet. 1:13-16)

How did Peter describe the old life of his readers? What behavior is expected of those who hope for Christ's coming? How do people today respond to calls to live holy lives?

1:13-16: Wherefore gird up the loins of your mind, be sober, and hope to the end for the grace that is to be brought unto you at the revelation of Jesus Christ; [14]as obedient children, not fashioning yourselves according to the former lusts in your ignorance: [15]but as he which hath called you is holy, so be ye holy in all manner of conversation; [16]because it is written, Be ye holy; for I am holy.

Two marks of the old, pre-Christian life are described in the last part of verse 14: **former lusts** and **ignorance.** This doesn't mean they were illiterate or mentally challenged. It means they did not know God or His Word. By secular standards, many non-Christians are well educated, but they do not have the key to truth that comes through Christian faith and experience. In their ignorance of the truth, they desire many things that are deadly to moral and spiritual life. The word for **lusts** is *epithumia.* It often refers to sexual lusts or passions, but at times refers to other worldly desires—such as greed for material things.

Verse 13 mentions two marks of Christians that stand over against these two sins. To counteract ignorance, believers are to **gird up the loins of your mind.** Many men wore long robes. Before running, they had to gather up the robes and tie them so their legs would not become tangled in their robes. They called this "girding up the loins." We might say, "Roll up your sleeves." Peter wanted his readers to think differently than they did in their time of ignorance.

Over against **lusts,** Peter wrote, **be sober** ("self-controlled," NIV; "self-disciplined," HCSB). In the New Testament, to be sober generally denotes self-control and the clarity of mind that goes with it. It is the opposite of living under the control of various lusts and passions. Such self-control is possible only as Christ works in your life.

The renewed mind and disciplined life are responses growing out of the experiences described in verses 1-12. The last part of verse 13 sums up a key theme in verses 1-12: **Hope to the end for the grace that is to be brought unto you at the revelation of Jesus Christ. To the end** translates *teleios,* which means "completely" (HCSB) or "fully" (NIV). In verses 1-12 we looked at several descriptions of the final stage of salvation at the Lord's future coming. Peter dealt at length on the coming day of the Lord in his second letter. He also dealt with the kind of people we ought to be if we truly believe in the Lord's coming. We should practice "holy conduct and godliness" (2 Pet. 3:11, HCSB).

Verses 13-14 have much in common with Romans 12:2: "Be not conformed to this world: but be ye transformed by the renewing of your mind." The word "conformed" is *suschematizo,* which is translated **fashioning** here in 1 Peter 1:14. Because we are **obedient children,** we must not conform our thoughts and actions to the standards of a lost world.

Verses 15-16 focus on the holy God and His expectation of holy living by His people. As we noted in the Word Study, the basic meaning for the word **holy** is "set apart." From that basic meaning came the meaning of moral holiness. Isaiah's vision of the holy God includes both the otherness of God, which sets Him apart as the unique God, and God's moral holiness, because Isaiah was convicted of his sins (Isa. 6:1-8). Any person or thing set apart by God is holy. For example, there was the holy city and holy implements for worship. When people are set apart by God, the moral aspect of holiness comes into being. Verse 16 contains a quotation of a basic Old Testament teaching from several verses in Leviticus (11:44-45; 19:2; 20:7). The context of these passages includes not only ceremonial cleansing but also righteous living.

How do people today feel about being **holy** as a personal goal? Do most Christians strive to be called holy? My own observation is that most people prefer not to be called holy. The plural of the word is translated "saints," but most people say, "I'm no saint." Yet the New Testament refers to each believer as a saint, in the sense that all believers are set apart to live holy lives.

What are the lasting truths in 1 Peter 1:13-16?

1. Christians are not to conform to their old, pre-Christian life of ignorance and lusts.

2. Believers are to have renewed minds and disciplined actions.

3. The hope of the Lord's coming exerts a moral imperative on believers.

4. As believers, we are to be holy because we worship a holy God.

Be Loving (1 Pet. 1:22-25)

Why are Christians to **love one another***? How are we to love one another? What is the role of God's Word?*

1:22-25: Seeing ye have purified your souls in obeying the truth through the Spirit unto unfeigned love of the brethren, see that ye love one another with a pure heart fervently: [23]being born again, not of corruptible seed, but of incorruptible, by the word of God, which liveth and abideth forever. [24]For all flesh is as grass, and all the glory of man as the flower of grass. The grass withereth, and the flower thereof falleth away: [25]but the word of the Lord endureth forever. And this is the word which by the gospel is preached unto you.

Christian experience is described in several ways in 1 Peter. The key idea is one introduced in 1:3. Christians are **born again.** Another way of describing what happens when we are born again is that we **purified** our **souls in obeying the truth through the Spirit.** People can be born again only through the Spirit. The truth and **the word of God** are instrumental in this spiritual miracle. Those who are born again become members of God's family. We become children of the God and Father of our Lord Jesus Christ. We discover that our Father has many children of all kinds of people. Out of love and gratitude for the loving Father—if for no other reason—we ought to love our brothers and sisters. If you were an orphan who was adopted by a rich, generous man, you would love your new father. Then you find a house full of other orphans whom he has adopted. Would you not strive to love all those whom your father loves? This is easier said than done because some of your new siblings are not easy to like.

Perhaps that is the reason Peter first described the need for **unfeigned love of the brethren. Unfeigned** translates *anupokritos,* from which we get our word *hypocrite,* except this word means "not hypocritical." In other words, it is to be "sincere love" (NIV, HCSB). The implication is that some love in the early churches was insincere. **Love of the brethren** translates *philadelphia,* which combines the word for warm family love with the word for brother. This shows that one aspect of loving one another in the church is developing a family spirit of mutual love. Paul advised Timothy to think of the church in this way. He would treat older men as fathers, older women as mothers, younger men as brothers, and younger women as sisters (1 Tim. 5: 1-2). Peter also used the usual word for Christian love, *agapao.* He told his readers to **love one another with a pure heart fervently.** Peter may have been using these two Greek words for love interchangeably, or he may have given a distinctive force to each one.

The word of God (v. 23) is the standard for all our faith and practice. Peter quoted the Scripture in verse 16 to call for holy living. The Word of God calls for us to love one another. Human life is short and uncertain, but God and His Word are eternal. If we live only for earthly things, we will leave everything behind or carry with us nothing, but if we respond to God and His **gospel,** we partake of what is eternal—**the word of the Lord endureth forever** (v. 25).

E. Stanley Jones was a missionary to India during the years when Mahatma Ghandi's influence was at its strongest. Jones described a conversation with Ghandi. He asked the Indian leader what Christians could do to make Christianity more effective in India. The answers he received apply to Christianity in any land. "I would suggest, first, that all of you Christians, missionaries and all, must begin to live more like Jesus Christ." "Second," Ghandi said, "I would suggest that you must practice your religion without adulterating or toning it down." "Third, I would suggest that you must put your emphasis upon love, for love is the center and soul of Christianity."[1]

What are the lasting lessons in 1 Peter 1:22-25?

1. Those who are born again become children of God.

2. Children of God are to love one another with a warm and sincere family love.

3. God's children are to practice self-giving love that acts for the good of others.

Be Mature (1 Pet. 2:1-3)

*What sins did Peter say to lay aside? Why is the Word of God so crucial in Christian growth? When do believers need the **milk of the word**? When do they need the meat of the Word? How do people find assurance that the Lord is good?*

2:1-3: **Wherefore laying aside all malice, and all guile, and hypocrisies, and envies, and all evil speakings, ²as newborn babes, desire the sincere milk of the word, that ye may grow thereby: ³if so be ye have tasted that the Lord is gracious.**

Laying aside is a picture of someone taking off and laying aside clothes that are dirty. Then Peter listed five sins that Christians should lay aside once for all. Unfortunately, these sins are among those of which church people often are guilty. These are "not the grosser vices of paganism, but community-destroying vices that are often tolerated by the modern church."[2] **Malice** is the word for "evil," but in this context it refers to ill will toward others. The word is often joined with grumbling, bitterness, and envy (see Eph. 4:31).

Guile is crafty "deceit" (NIV, HCSB). This word also is found in verse 22 and in 3:10, where it refers to speaking or acting from selfish motives. This sin never speaks the full and honest truth unless this would benefit the speaker.

Hypocrisies are what Ghandi pointed to when he advised Christians to live like Jesus Christ. Peter had in mind the insincerity and pretense of professing Jesus but only playing at being a Christian in how we live.

Envies refers to all the desires to have what someone else has. This applies not only to material things but also to praise or prestige. Envy often is the hidden root of the other sins. Envious people have malice toward those who receive more recognition than they do. This leads to deceit and hypocrisy.

Evil speakings focuses on "slander" (NIV, HCSB) or its more common form, "gossip." This may be the leading form of evil speech by church members. It is the opposite of "speaking the truth in love" (Eph. 4:15). "Deceit is practiced to a person's face, when one speaks only nicely of him or her, but for the person with envy and malice within, the insincerity will come out as he or she criticizes the person to others in that person's absence. Whether this criticism is cloaked as 'sharing a problem,' a 'prayer request,' or a 'concern,' it makes little difference."[3]

Newborn babes uses the word *brephos* for **babes** ("babies," NIV; "infants," HCSB). This word is used in Luke 2:16 of the baby Jesus in the manger. Here it refers to new converts to Christ. The word for **desire** is a strong word, consistent with the analogy of an infant's desire for **milk.** An infant must have milk to survive and to grow. In the same way, moral and spiritual growth is dependent on a diet of the Word of God. Many ancient copies of 1 Peter end verse 2 after **that ye may grow thereby**

with the Greek words *eis soterian* ("in salvation," NIV, HCSB). In 1 Peter 1:5,9,10 salvation is mentioned. We noted that after being saved from sin's penalty we are being saved from sin's power and moving toward Christ's coming when we shall be saved from sin's presence. The Word of God is crucial in each stage of salvation. It convicts and converts sinners to salvation, and it causes believers to grow toward maturity in Christ.

This helps explain the reason the Bible is necessary at each stage of our lives. For one thing, it is the moral yardstick by which we see our sins and shortcomings. Christians who continually expose their lives to God's Word have the spotlight of divine truth turned on sins like those listed in verse 1. Positively, the Word nourishes us spiritually as God speaks to us. Find a mature Christian, and you can be sure this person lives in and by God's Word.

We never outgrow our need for the Word of God. Paul rebuked some members of the Corinthian church for their sinful actions. He said they were like babies who could be fed only with the milk of the Word, not with its meat (1 Cor. 3:1-4). Hebrews 5:11-14 makes a similar charge. The *milk* of the Word is appropriate for new believers, but we need to grow to the point where we can be nourished on the *meat* of the Word.

Among the ways Peter showed the importance of the Word of God were His many quotations and allusions to the Scriptures. We saw Old Testament quotations in 1:16,24-25. Verse 3 is another quotation— this time from Psalm 34:8. The word **if** has the force of "since" in verse 3. **Gracious** refers to the Lord's goodness. Thus, **If so be ye have tasted that the Lord is gracious** can be translated "since you have tasted that the Lord is good" (HCSB). **Tasted** means to experience for yourself. Believers have experienced the goodness of the Lord.

What are the lasting lessons in 1 Peter 2:1-3?

1. Christians should lay aside their sins as they would take off dirty clothes.

2. Church members need to get rid of sins such as ill will, deceit, hypocrisy, envy, and gossip.

3. New believers need the Word of God the way an infant needs milk.

4. The Word of God nurtures growth in Christ as long as we live.

Be Honorable (1 Pet. 2:11-12)

*In what sense are Christians **strangers and pilgrims**? In what sense is Christianity a "counter culture"? What accusations and suspicions* *did pagans have about believers? How are Christians to respond to slander, prejudice, and misunderstandings by non-Christians?*

2:11-12: Dearly beloved, I beseech you as strangers and pilgrims, abstain from fleshly lusts, which war against the soul; [12]having your conversation honest among the Gentiles: that, whereas they speak against you as evildoers, they may by your good works, which they shall behold, glorify God in the day of visitation.

There are two keys to unlock the message of these verses. One is the fact that Christians are **strangers and pilgrims** on earth. Two Greek words similar in meaning are put together. Both refer to people whose true home is in heaven and who see earthly life as temporary. If there is any difference in meaning, the first word *(paroikos)* refers to foreigners who reside for a time in a foreign land, and the second word *(parepidemos)* refers to people who are just passing through a foreign land. The *Holman Christian Standard Bible* calls them "aliens and temporary residents." People who live by the world's standards follow the ways of a society who does not know God or His ways. In a sense, Christian standards—like those in God's Word—represent a kind of "counter culture" that is often misunderstood by people of the world.

The second key to verses 11-12 is the fact that at the time Peter wrote most people knew little about Christians and some spoke **against** them **as evildoers.** One of Peter's purposes in writing was to seek to counteract slanderous accusations against Christians in first-century pagan society. Christianity was a new religion, and outsiders often spread false accusations against members of this minority movement. Pagan people heard certain things about Christians and twisted what they heard into false accusations. Because Christians rejected the ancient gods, they were considered atheists. Because they spoke of Christ as King of a kingdom, they were suspected of anarchy. Pagans heard that Christians had "love feasts" and often spoke about loving one another, and they accused them of immorality. They heard believers quoting Jesus' words about the Lord's Supper and accused them of cannibalism.

How are Christians to respond to false accusations? Peter emphasized the need for Christians to show by their actions the kind of people they truly are. The word **conversation** translates *anastrophe*, which refers to one's way of living, not just to what one says. **Honest** is a word that refers to goodness that is beautiful. "Conduct yourselves honorably among the Gentiles" (HCSB); "Always let others see you behaving properly," (CEV).

Peter mentioned a negative and a positive way to live honorably. Negatively, he stated, **Abstain from fleshly lusts which war against the soul.** The way to silence accusations of sexual immorality is to avoid any form of this sin by attacking its root system of **lusts.** On a positive note, a life of **good works** may lead pagan critics eventually to **glorify God.**

What are the lasting lessons in 1 Peter 2:11-12?

1. Christians live in the world but must not be of the world.

2. Non-Christians sometimes view Christians with suspicion and prejudice.

3. Christians should respond to criticisms by living consistently and honorably.

❖ *Spiritual Transformations*

We are to live holy lives because our God is holy. Ignorance and lusts are to be replaced by renewed minds and disciplined actions. Because we have been born into God's family, we are to love one another with sincere family love and with self-giving love. Such love demands that we lay aside sins of ill will, pretense, hypocrisy, envy, and gossip. New converts ought to desire the Word of God the way an infant desires milk. As God's children, we are to live by the standards of God's eternal kingdom. Sometimes we will be regarded with suspicion and prejudice by worldly people, but we should live in such a way that our critics may come to glorify God.

"Practice what you preach (profess)" is what every Christian must do. Failing to live consistently with our professed beliefs is hypocrisy, and nothing is so deadly to the cause of Christ. On the other hand, Christians who live holy lives, love one another, obey the Word of God, and live by eternal standards may have the joy of leading critics to glorify our God.

In which of the four areas of Christian living on the Scripture Outline are you closest to doing what God's Word calls for? _____

In which area are you the furthest away from obeying the Lord? How can you improve in this area? _____

Prayer of Commitment: Lord, help me live in such a way that those who criticize Christians will come to glorify You. Amen.

[1]E. Stanley Jones, *The Christ of the Indian Road* [New York: The Abingdon Press, 1925], 126-127.
[2]Peter H. Davids, *The First Epistle of Peter,* in The New International Commentary on the New Testament [Grand Rapids: William B. Eerdmans Publishing Company, 1990], 80.
[3]Davids, *The First Epistle of Peter,* 81.

BE HUMBLE

Background Passages: 1 Peter 2:13–3:12; 5:5-7
Focal Passages: 1 Peter 2:13-14,17-21; 3:1-4,7-9; 5:5-7
Key Verse: 1 Peter 2:21

❖ *Significance of the Lesson*

• The *Theme* of this lesson is that successful living includes practicing humility.
• The *Life Question* addressed in this lesson is, How should I demonstrate humility?
• The *Biblical Truth* is that humility, which includes having a proper perspective of one's responsibilities toward God and toward others, is an essential ingredient for living a successful and fulfilled life.
• The *Life Impact* is to help you live humbly.

Views About Humility

With few exceptions, today's culture encourages people to focus on themselves and on fulfilling their own desires rather than on others and meeting others' needs. In such a culture, believers who exercise genuine humility are in the minority. Pride, not humility, is more natural for most people. Exercising true humility is possible only through God's grace and power.

Word Study: *Humility, humble*

The noun *tapeinophrosune* ("humility"), the related verb *tapeinoo* ("be humble"), and the adjective *tapeinos* ("humble") all appear in 1 Peter 5:5-6. The basic meaning of the verb is "to make low." It is used literally in Luke 3:5 of lowering a mountain. Normally the word is used figuratively: sometimes in the negative sense of humiliate, sometimes in the positive sense of being humble. In Greek usage, the word nearly always had a negative connotation. Humility was not seen as a virtue among the Greeks. In fact, the Greeks used words of this family to refer to people who were groveling, slavish, and mean-spirited. Christ, and the early Christians following Him, redeemed these words to describe a basic Christian virtue. Jesus even used the adjective to describe Himself as "lowly" in heart (Matt. 11:29). Truly He lived a life of humble, self-giving service to others and left us an example to follow in His steps.

❖ *Search the Scriptures*

According to Peter, an illustration of demonstrating humility is humble submission to government authorities; another is for servants to humbly submit to their masters. Christ set the example for others by patiently suffering abuse. Christian wives are to humbly submit themselves to their husbands and seek to win lost husbands by how they live. Christian husbands are to treat their wives as joint heirs of God's grace. Showing compassion by giving good for evil is an expression of humility. Humbling oneself before God is the heart of humility.

The following five outline points answer the Life Question.

Submit to Authorities (1 Pet. 2:13-14,17-19)

To whom are Christians to submit themselves? How were these verses used to justify the divine right of kings and slavery?

2:13-14,17-19: Submit yourselves to every ordinance of man for the Lord's sake: whether it be to the king, as supreme; [14]or unto governors, as unto them that are sent by him for the punishment of evildoers, and for the praise of them that do well.

. . . .

[17]Honor all men. Love the brotherhood. Fear God. Honor the king. [18]Servants, be subject to your masters with all fear; not only to the good and gentle, but also to the froward. [19]For this is thankworthy, if a man for conscience toward God endure grief, suffering wrongfully.

The Greek word *hupotasso* is a key word in this passage. Peter and Paul both used this word to describe the voluntary submission of Christians to government authority (1 Pet. 2:13; Rom. 13:1,5), of slaves to their masters (1 Pet. 2:18; Titus 2:9), of wives to their husbands (1 Pet. 3:1,5; Eph. 5:24; Col. 3:18), and of Christians to one another (1 Pet. 5:5; Eph. 5:21). In the New Testament the word is used in the active voice of God subjecting people and things to himself. The middle and the passive voice, however, describe a voluntary submission. This is true whether it is translated **submit yourselves** (2:13; 5:5), **be subject to** (2:18), or **be in subjection to** (3:1,5). Thus submitting yourself to another person is always a voluntary act, although in the biblical examples just named it is done in obedience to God's will. This is seen in the words **for the Lord's sake** (2:13).

Kenneth Wuest tells us, "The words 'submit yourselves' are the translation of a Greek military term meaning 'to arrange in military fashion under the command of a leader.'"[1] Thus submitting oneself is based on recognizing and respecting authority. Most translators assume **every ordinance of man** refers to "every human institution" (HCSB) or "every authority instituted among men" (NIV). The other words show that Peter had in mind the authority of government. He mentioned submission **to the king, as supreme** and **unto governors, as unto them that are sent by him.** Peter did not spell out what Paul made clear in Romans 13:1-7—that the idea of government was instituted by God, but this is implied in the purpose statement **for the punishment of evildoers, and for the praise of them that do well.** Before we leave this verse we should note that God did not establish any one form of government as the only one. Rather, He established the principle that people organize to provide an orderly society.

In verse 17 Peter summarized how Christians should relate to a broad range of groups. In **honor all men, honor** refers to respect that looks at the worthy qualities of others. This is one expression of Christian humility. Pride seeks honor for ourselves. We push ourselves forward as those most deserving honor. Humble people push forward others. It is noteworthy that the same word used of the king in this verse is used for all people. It is also important to see that the word **fear** is used in verse 17 only of **God. Love** describes how Christians are to treat brothers in the Lord.

In this passage Peter also addressed **servants** who worked in the household (the Greek word *oiketai* comes from *oikos,* "house"). This included not only cooks, maids, and other domestic servants but also slaves who served as nurses and tutors for children. (Paul used the general word for slave, *doulos.*) The churches had many members who were slaves. In Ephesians 6:5-9 Paul addressed both slaves and masters, but Peter wrote to Christian slaves of non-Christian masters. Peter said that slaves should submit not only to their masters who were **good and gentle** but also to those who were **froward** ("cruel," HCSB; "harsh," NIV). The word Peter used for **masters** is *despotais*, from which we get our word *despots*. Peter told Christian slaves to submit themselves even to harsh masters, "for it is commendable if a man bears up under the pain of unjust suffering because he is conscious of God" (NIV).

Why did Peter and Paul not attack such an obviously evil institution as slavery? One reason was because Christ came first of all to save people from sin and death. He refused to become an earthly king. Another reason was because Christianity lacked any power to change such things without bringing down on believers and slaves massive, brutal repression. The slave rebellion under Spartacus had been punished without mercy. Yet keep in mind two important facts: (1) Christ gave new endurance to enslaved people. (2) Christianity sowed the seeds that finally led to the abolition of slavery and to greater political freedom.

Freedom brings even greater responsibility for Christians to fear God, love one another, and honor all people, including those is government and law enforcement.

What are some of the lasting lessons in 1 Peter 2:13-14,17-19?

1. Christians are to submit themselves to those whom God places in authority over them.

2. This applies to government, which has the responsibility of punishing evildoers and rewarding those who do right.

3. Proud people seek honor for themselves; humble people seek to honor others.

4. Living as free people in a free society calls for greater personal responsibility.

Imitate Christ (1 Pet. 2:20-21)

In what way did slaves sometimes experience part of what Christ experienced? In what way is the cross of Christ more than an example? In what way is it an example?

2:20-21: For what glory is it, if, when ye be buffeted for your faults, ye shall take it patiently? but if, when ye do well, and suffer for it, ye take it patiently, this is acceptable with God. [21]For even hereunto were ye called: because Christ also suffered for us, leaving us an example, that ye should follow his steps.

In verses 20-21 Peter continued to speak about slaves submitting themselves to their masters, even to cruel masters. In verse 20 he described two situations in which a master would beat his slave. In one scenario, a slave did something wrong and was **buffeted** for his **faults.** In the other scenario, a slave was unjustly beaten. He did nothing, but his evil master beat him. Suppose both slaves endured their beatings with patience. The first slave deserved his punishment; the second did not. Peter concluded that God is pleased with the slave who **patiently** endured his unjust treatment.

Peter drew this conclusion because he saw in the patient endurance of unjust treatment a picture of what Jesus voluntarily endured when He suffered unjustly. Christians are **called,** Peter reminded his readers, to live as Jesus lived and died—**Christ also suffered for us, leaving us an example. Example** literally means "writing under." "It was used of words given children to copy, both as a writing exercise and as a means of impressing a moral. Sometimes it was used with reference to the act of tracing over written letters. Peter changes over easily from the idea of a child tracing over the writing of the writing-master to a Christian planting his feet in the foot-prints left by our Lord."[2]

In verses 22-25 Peter showed that Jesus' death was much more than a good example for us to follow. When Peter wrote, He "bare our sins in his own body on the tree" and "by whose stripes ye were healed" (v. 24), he obviously had in mind Isaiah's account of the Suffering Servant in Isaiah 53. The fact that Jesus died to save us from our sins does not deny that He also died to set an example of how saved people are to live and die. Jesus calls for followers who will deny themselves, take up their cross, and follow Him (Matt. 16:24). Those who know Him **should follow his steps.**

Patiently enduring unjust punishment is only one way of living by the way of the cross and the resurrection. Anytime we put the will of God and the needs of others before our own needs and do so at some cost, we are following the Lord in the way of the cross. The cross is not only the door to the Christian life but also the way of the Christian life. This way is the way of humble self-giving love.

What are the lasting lessons in 1 Peter 2:20-21?

1. Jesus suffered unjustly in order to die for our sins, but in so doing He set an example for us to follow.

2. As Christians we are to follow Jesus' example in submitting to unjust treatment if need be.

Honor Your Spouse (1 Pet. 3:1-4,7)

How can a woman be a Christian and be married to a non-Christian husband? In what ways should a Christian wife submit herself to a non-Christian husband? What principles do Peter's instructions about women's hairstyles and fashions teach us day? How did Christ elevate the place of women?

3:1-4,7: Likewise, ye wives, be in subjection to your own husbands; that, if any obey not the word, they also may without the word be won by the conversation of the wives; [2]while they behold your chaste conversation coupled with fear. [3]whose adorning let it not be that outward adorning of plaiting the hair, and of wearing of gold, or of putting on of apparel; [4]but let it be the hidden man of the heart, in that which is not corruptible, even the ornament of a meek and quiet spirit, which is in the sight of God of great price.

. . . .

[7]Likewise, ye husbands, dwell with them according to knowledge, giving honor unto the wife, as unto the weaker vessel, and as being heirs together of the grace of life; that your prayers be not hindered.

Peter addressed verses 1-4 to Christian wives with non-Christian husbands. Since believers were taught to marry only fellow believers (1 Cor. 7:39; 2 Cor. 6:14), most of these situations occurred when the wife in a non-Christian marriage was converted but her husband was not. Regardless of whether their husbands were Christians, Peter instructed **wives** to **be in subjection to your own husbands.** Peter used the same word that he used to describe the voluntary submission of citizens to the government and of slaves to their masters. The word is never used of the husband forcibly subjecting his wife. It is a voluntary submission, but such submission is the plan of God for marriage.

If any obey not the word was Peter's way of describing a non-Christian husband. Peter told Christian wives to stay with unbelieving husbands in order that **they also may without the word be won by the conversation of the wives.** This is another example of the word **conversation** referring not to words but to her whole way of life. In fact, Peter emphasized seeking to win the unbelieving partner "without words" (NIV). Hopefully, unsaved husbands would be led to Christ "by the way their wives live, when they observe your pure, reverent lives" (HCSB).

Peter gave one illustration of what he meant. He said that Christian wives should be noted for the "inner beauty" of "a gentle and quiet spirit" (HCSB). He contrasted such beauty of spirit with the kind of beauty many non-Christian women sought: "Your beauty should not be the outer beauty of elaborate hairstyles and the wearing of gold ornaments or of fine clothes" (HCSB). This instruction doesn't mean that a Christian woman should not seek to look her best. The abiding principles, as verse 4 shows, are for Christian women to stress their character rather than their appearance and to avoid seeking to look many of the ways non-Christians consider stylish.

Peter addressed verse 7 to Christian **husbands.** This is the only time the word translated **dwell with** is used in the New Testament, but it appears eight times in the Septuagint (the Greek translation of the Old Testament), where it often included living together in sexual oneness. The word thus teaches that a Christian husband is to be faithful to his lifetime commitment to his wife. **Knowledge** has the ideas of understanding and consideration.

Christian husbands also are to give **honor unto the wife, as unto the weaker vessel.** The use of **weaker** here refers only to physical strength—"she isn't as strong as you are" (CEV). **Honor** means to affirm her value and worth. The last part of verse 7 adds further positive aspects of Christian marriage. Although the wife recognizes the husband's leadership role, he recognizes that they are **heirs together of the grace of life.** There is no hint of any inferiority; both are joint heirs of the same grace of God.

Some people accuse Christianity of demeaning women. The opposite is true. Jesus and His teachings elevated women, who were treated almost as non-persons in ancient Greco-Roman society.

What are some of the lasting lessons in 1 Peter 3:1-4 and 7?

1. Christian wives voluntarily submit themselves to their husbands.

2. Christian wives in a non-Christian marriage should seek to win their husbands by how they live.

3. Christian husbands are to be faithful, understanding, and considerate of wives who are joint heirs of the grace of life.

4. Ancient society demeaned women; Christianity elevated women.

Show Compassion (1 Pet. 3:8-9)

What characteristics should be true of all believers? How do these qualities express humility?

3:8-9: Finally, be ye all of one mind, having compassion one of another, love as brethren, be pitiful, be courteous: [9]not rendering evil for evil, or railing for railing: but contrariwise blessing; knowing that ye are thereunto called, that ye should inherit a blessing.

The word **finally** doesn't mean the end of the letter but refers to the concluding words of one section. Peter had addressed several different groups, but these closing words were for **all** his readers. Peter listed six qualities that should be true for all believers. First, they all were to be **of one mind**. The believers represented different groups within society: slaves, wives, husbands, and so forth. Yet all of these were one in Christ, the source of their oneness of spirit.

Compassion translates *sympatheis,* the word from which we get our word *sympathy.* To be "sympathetic" (NIV, HCSB) is to feel what someone else feels. Christians should "rejoice with them that do rejoice, and weep with them that weep" (Rom. 12:15). This is how members of the same family feel. Third, they were to **love as brethren.** This translates *philadelphia,* "brotherly love." **Be pitiful** translates a word that literally referred to internal organs of the body. The Greeks used this word to describe courage. Jews used it to describe affection and feeling. Thus "compassionate" (NIV, HCSB) or "kindhearted" (NASB) communicates the meaning today.

Some manuscripts, such as those the *King James Version* follows, next have a word meaning **courteous.** Others manuscripts have *tapeinophron,* the word meaning "humble" (NIV, HCSB), "humble minded" (see the NRSV), or "humble in spirit" (NASB). This word is kin to the three words found in 1 Peter 5:5-7 (see the Word Study). The Greeks did not consider humility a virtue. In spite of 20 centuries of Christian influence, people still give mostly lip service to a humble spirit. The way of most people is putting self first, but Christ calls us to put God and others before ourselves. Each of us is "not to think of himself more highly than he ought to think" (Rom. 12:3). In fact, Paul went a step further when he wrote: "Do nothing out of rivalry or conceit, but in humility consider others as more important than your-selves" (Phil. 2:3, HCSB). Jesus set the example for humility when He washed the disciples' feet (John 13:1-15). The cross, of course, is the ultimate expression of selfless humility (Phil. 2:5-8).

In verse 9 Peter focused on how Christians are to respond to persecution by non-Christians. Unbelievers treated Peter's readers badly and insulted them with words. The normal response of most people would be to hurt those who have hurt them. But Jesus did not do this. Instead, He silently bore the insults and blows as well as the humiliating and painful death of crucifixion. Therefore, Jesus' followers were instructed not to give back **evil for evil, or railing for railing** ("insult for insult," HCSB). Instead of giving back what we receive, we are to give a **blessing.** This involves not only good words but good actions toward our tormentors. Paul elaborated on this same point in Romans 12:17-21. Those who become channels of blessing **inherit a blessing.**

What are the lasting lessons in 1 Peter 3:8-9?

1. All Christians should evidence oneness of spirit, sympathy, love for one another, compassion, humility, and blessing to all.

2. Toward their persecutors, believers should not return evil for evil but good for evil.

Depend on God (1 Pet. 5:5-7)

*What does it mean to be humble toward one another? Why is pride the opposite of humility? What does it mean to humble ourselves before God? What kind of **care** are we to cast upon God?*

5:5-7: Likewise, ye younger, submit yourselves unto the elder. Yea, all of you be subject one to another, and be clothed with humility: for God resisteth the proud, and giveth grace to the humble. ⁶Humble yourselves therefore under the mighty hand of God, that he may exalt you in due time: ⁷casting all your care upon him; for he careth for you.

Peter added to his list of those who submit themselves. **Younger** believers were to **submit** themselves **unto the elder** ones ("those who are older," NIV). In verses 1-4 Peter had been writing about church leaders as elders, but in verse 5 he wrote about elderly people in general. The Jews honored and respected their parents and other older people; so should Christians.

The words **one to another** may go with either **be subject** or with **be clothed with humility.** If it is the former, as in the *King James Version*, Peter was teaching the same thing as what Paul wrote in

Ephesians 5:21. Most translations, however, put these words with **be clothed with humility:** "Clothe yourselves with humility toward one another" (NASB, NIV, HCSB). Since voluntary submission is an expression of humility, we can conclude that all of us are to relate to one another with humility.

Peter quoted Proverbs 3:34 in verse 5. In the Old Testament **the proud** were arrogant toward man and God. Pride is the opposite of humility. Pride includes an attitude that puts self before others, even before God. Being **humble** involves placing ourselves under God's sovereign control and seeing others as people of worth in God's eyes. God opposes and finally brings down arrogant people. Because the humble are open to God, He can pour out His **grace** on them. Jesus' parable of the tax collector and the Pharisee illustrates how a proud man excluded himself and a humble man received divine grace (Luke 18:9-14).

Peter concluded from this that people of faith should **humble** themselves **under the mighty hand of God** because He will **exalt** them **in due time.** Keep in mind that Peter wrote to Christians who were being persecuted by proud, arrogant people. At such times even people of strong faith sometimes wonder why God allows this and how long will it continue. Peter's answer was that they should yield themselves to God. His **mighty hand** will rectify the situation in His own time and way. Meanwhile, as they yield to God's power, they should know that God cares for them—**Casting all your care** ("anxiety," NASB, NIV, NRSV) **upon him; for he careth for you.** In times of trouble, our worries and fears multiply. The antidote for worldly anxiety is humble submission to Almighty God and trust in His goodness.

What are the lasting lessons in 1 Peter 5:5-7?

1. Pride is arrogance against God and others.

2. Humility involves humbling ourselves toward God and others.

3. During difficult times, yield to God's power and entrust yourself to His care.

❖ Spiritual Transformations

Peter called on Christians to submit themselves to governing authorities. He instructed Christian slaves to submit even to harsh masters. This involved suffering unjustly—as Jesus did, thus providing salvation and an example for saved people. Christian wives are to submit themselves to their husbands and seek to win non-Christian husbands by how they live. Christian husbands are to treat their wives as joint heirs of God's grace. All believers are to have one mind, sympathy, love, compassion, humility, and bring blessing to others. They are to give back good for evil. Younger Christians are to submit themselves to older ones. All are to relate to one another in humility. In good times and in bad, believers are to humble themselves before God and cast their worries on Him.

In this Study Theme, we are looking at "Peter's Principles for Successful Living." Humility was one of his key principles. In modern books and workshops about successful living, humility is probably not even mentioned. If it is mentioned, it is listed as the opposite to an aggressive drive for recognition and advancement. Humility is equated with a lack of self-confidence and ambition.

How do you think Peter would respond to this outlook? _____
_____

Humility is a very subtle quality. We are in constant danger of becoming proud of our humility. We become like the proverbial person who wrote a book on "My Humility and How I Attained It." *How can you tell if a person is genuinely humble?* _____

How would you rate your level of humility? _____

Prayer of Commitment: Lord, help me follow in Your steps by living for You and for others. Amen.

[1]Wuest, *First Peter*, 60.
[2]Wuest, *First Peter*, 67.

TAKE COURAGE

Background Passage: 1 Peter 3:13–4:6,12-19
Focal Passages: 1 Peter 3:13-17; 4:1-3,12-16,19
Key Verse: 1 Peter 3:15

❖ *Significance of the Lesson*

• The *Theme* of this lesson is that successful living includes faithfulness and courage in the midst of suffering.
• The *Life Question* this lesson addresses is, How can I show faithfulness and courage, even when my allegiance to Christ is ridiculed?
• The *Biblical Truth* is that God enables believers to stand faithfully and courageously for Him, even when their allegiance to Christ is ridiculed.
• The *Life Impact* is to help you show faithfulness and courage in your allegiance to Christ.

Opposition to Christianity

One of the ironies of contemporary culture is intolerance against Christianity in a culture that claims to be tolerant. One reason for this is Christianity's belief in moral and spiritual absolutes. Secular culture insists that absolutes do not exist. Everything is relative to time, place, and people. Because Christians stand for absolute truth, a relativistic culture considers them old-fashioned and out of step with modern thought. Christians are now greatly misunderstood in our land. This failure to understand leads at times to ridicule and rejection, similar to that endured by some first-century Christians. In this face of such ridicule and rejection, Christians need to take courage.

Word Study: *Reproached*

The word *oneidizo* means "reproach," "revile," or "heap abuse on." Jesus was reviled as He hung on the cross (Mark 15:32). He predicted the same for His followers (Matt. 5:11). In 1 Peter 4:14 the apostle told his readers that if they were **reproached** ("insulted," NIV; "ridiculed," HCSB; "reviled," NASB, NRSV) for the name of Jesus, they were blessed.

❖ *Search the Scriptures*

Peter told his readers to be ready to explain their hope to anyone who asked. Since Christ caused believers to die to sin, Christians are to leave the sins of the past. Christians should not be ashamed of suffering as followers of Christ. If believers suffer according to God's will, they can do right and trust God.

Be Ready to Defend Your Faith (1 Pet. 3:13-17)

How do verses 13-14 present the ideal and the actual? Do verses 15-17 reflect a formal trial or an informal inquiry? How do these verses apply to all Christians?

3:13-17: And who is he that will harm you, if ye be followers of that which is good? [14]But and if ye suffer for righteousness' sake, happy are ye: and be not afraid of their terror, neither be troubled; [15]but sanctify the Lord God in your hearts: and be ready always to give an answer to every man that asketh you a reason of the hope that is in you with meekness and fear: [16]having a good conscience; that, whereas they speak evil of you, as of evildoers, they may be ashamed that falsely accuse your good conversation in Christ. [17]For it is better, if the will of God be so, that ye suffer for well-doing, than for evildoing.

Peter at this point in his letter dealt in more detail with persecution. He had begun with general references to trials (1:6-7). Along the way he had written about the slanders they endured (2:12; 3:9). Beginning with 3:13-17, Peter dealt more directly with the situation his readers were facing.

Verse 13 can be understood in two ways—both of which are true. Peter may have been stating the way things ought to be in a just society. Earlier, Peter stressed that God's intention for government is that it punish those who do wrong and reward those who do right (2:14). If all people had such a government, **who is he that will harm you, if ye be followers of that which is good?** If this was Peter's point, he was stating how things ought to be, and in verse 14 he contrasted the ideal with the way things actually were.

The other interpretation of verse 13 emphasizes the word **harm.** According to this view, Peter was using the word in a special way— of ultimate and eternal harm. If a person does what is right in God's eyes, persecutors cannot harm the person in an ultimate way. For example, Jesus predicted that some would be put to death for His sake, but He said, "There shall not a hair of your head perish" (Luke 21:18). J. N. D. Kelly, who holds this view, wrote, Peter "is not deluding his correspondents with the idea that, if their conduct is beyond reproach, they will escape abuse, maltreatment, physical injury; he has already conceded the possibility in 2:20. His point is that, whatever disasters strike the man of faith, they cannot touch the integrity of his personality or injure him in the ultimate sense."[1]

The first part of verse 14 paraphrases Jesus' teaching—"Blessed are they which are persecuted for righteousness' sake" (Matt. 5:10). In an ideal world righteousness would be rewarded; but in a sinful world, good and godly people suffer for their faith and way of life. Yet by the standards of God's kingdom such people are **happy** or "blessed" (NIV, HCSB).

Isaiah 8:12 is reflected in verse 14b. A literal translation of verse 14b is "Do not fear what they fear" (NIV, HCSB). Many interpret this to mean, "Be not affected with fear by the fear which they strive to inspire in your heart"[2] or "Do not fear their intimidation" (NASB). The normal response to persecution is fear and anxiety, but Christians are to face it with courage and confidence.

Isaiah 8:13 is reflected in verse 15. Some copies of 1 Peter, such as those followed by the *King James Version,* have **but sanctify the Lord God in your hearts.** Other copies have "but sanctify Christ as Lord in your hearts" (NASB; similarly, NIV, HCSB). **Sanctify** means "set apart" (NIV, HCSB). Instead of having fears and worries, Christians should commit themselves totally to Jesus Christ as Lord.

The key word in verse 15 is **answer.** This word *(apologia)* was at times used of a defendant's answer in a formal court case. The normal meaning of this word is "defense," and the meaning of the related verb is "to speak in one's defense." Both words often referred to defending oneself against the charge of being a Christian. Translators are divided about whether to translate the word here as **answer** (KJV, NIV, CEV) or "defense" (NEB, REB, NASB, NRSV, HCSB).

Based on this, some Bible students emphasize verse 15 as evidence that the persecution faced by Peter's readers included formal accusations against Christians by the government. This was certainly true by the early second century, but it was not the usual situation before the persecution by Nero. However, early believers such as Peter and Paul were challenged to defend themselves before various groups. Therefore, what Peter wrote applies to such times. Christians in many places in the world today face such trials.

The other meaning of the word was not an answer to a formal accusation in a court but an answer to a question asked by a person or group. Christians are to **be ready always to give an answer to every man that asketh . . . a reason of the hope that is in** them. I believe that the words **always** and **every man** show that the situation was different from a formal trial. In other words, Christians were sometimes asked to explain what they believed and why to a variety of people, not just to judges. This applies to all believers in any generation, including our own.

Apologetics is a technical name for stating why Christians believe as they do. We do not *apologize* for our faith, but we seek to state the strongest intellectual arguments for the faith. Peter's words apply to all believers. Each of us has opportunities to explain to unbelievers what we believe and why we believe it. When asked, we ought to give **a reason** for our faith. This kind of witness can be effective, especially if we are answering someone's question. The answer should be personal, reasonable, and Christ-centered. Peter wrote that you should **be ready always** to respond to opportunities to explain **the hope that is in you.**

Notice that Peter used the word **hope** instead of *faith.* He considered the living hope based on Christ's resurrection and the believer's new birth to be central in giving assurance to believers. He probably also knew that one of Christianity's strongest appeals in the pagan world was its promise of eternal hope (1:3-12).

Meekness ("gentleness," NIV, HCSB) **and fear** ("respect," NIV, HCSB) describe the spirit in which the testimony is given. Both attitudes may refer to our attitude to those to whom we witness. Or the second response may refer to our reverent fear of God. Keep in mind that the believers were slandered by some people in that day. Christians needed to be sure that their lives were positive testimonies for the Lord. These slandered Christians should have **a good conscience** because the charges and rumors about them were false. They were not **evildoers** as their critics claimed. The hoped-for result of this approach was that their critics would **be ashamed** because the critics' slanders proved to be untrue. This applies today to the importance of Christians living consistent lives. If a professing Christian does not live a Christian life, no one will pay attention to the person's verbal testimony. If God's will is that we **suffer** at the hands of others, we must be sure it is **for well-doing,** not **for evildoing.**

What are the lasting lessons in 1 Peter 3:13-17?

1. In an ideal world, good people would be rewarded and evil people punished; however, in our imperfect world some people suffer for righteousness' sake.

2. Christians should face persecution with courage and confidence, not fear and anxiety.

3. Christians always should be ready to explain why they are Christians.

4. Their testimony should be personal, reasonable, and Christ-centered.

5. The attitude of a Christian witness should be gentle and respectful.

6. The life of a Christian witness should be consistent with faith in Christ.

Remember Christ's Example (1 Pet. 4:1-3)

Why is this a hard passage to translate and understand? What clear truths are taught in these verses?

4:1-3: Forasmuch then as Christ hath suffered for us in the flesh, arm yourselves likewise with the same mind: for he that hath suffered in the flesh hath ceased from sin; ²that he no longer should live the rest of his time in the flesh to the lusts of men, but to the will of God. ³For the time past of our life may suffice us to have wrought the will of the Gentiles, when we walked in lasciviousness, lusts, excess of wine, revelings, banquetings, and abominable idolatries.

This is one of the more difficult passages in 1 Peter. It in turn is part of a larger passage that ranks among the most difficult in the New Testament (3:18–4:6). Two teachings are crystal clear in 4:1-3. One is the fact that **Christ hath suffered for us in the flesh.** First Peter 3:18a states the heart of the gospel: "For Christ also hath once suffered for sins, the just for the unjust, that he might bring us to God." The other clear truth is that the sins of the old life must be left behind (v. 3). The difficulty is understanding the last part of verse 1 and verse 2. Who is he that **hath ceased from sin**? Many Bible students believe that Peter was still referring to the One who **suffered for us in the flesh.** If this is so, then in what sense did Jesus cease from sin? The *Holman Christian Standard Bible* has, "the One who suffered in the flesh has finished with sin." Other Bible students believe the words refer to anyone who has overcome suffering. The *New Revised Standard Version* has this parenthetical insert in verse 1, "(for whoever has suffered in the flesh has finished with sin)."

Those who believe Jesus **ceased from sin** have to explain these words. "'To finish with' *(pauesthai),* it should be noted, does not necessarily imply active personal participation with that in which one **has finished.**"[3] However, "ceasing from sin" is not the usual way the Bible describes Jesus and sin. Probably we should understand 1 Peter 4:1b in light of other teachings. We know, for example, that He wrestled with temptation and as a result of overcoming that temptation is able to help us when we are tempted (Heb. 2:18; 4:15). He defeated sin by refusing to yield to it personally, and He finished God's redemptive plan of salvation from sin (Luke 24:46-48; John 19:30). He comes into the lives of believers to enable us to die to sin (Rom. 6:3-4; Gal. 2:20). Thus Christ ceased from sin by His perfect life and atoning death. He enables believers to cease from sin by saving us and empowering us.

The words **arm yourselves likewise with the same mind** provide a pathway from Christ finishing with sin to believers finishing with sin. Some Bible students think that **he** in verse 2 also refers to Jesus. If so, **the lusts of men** refers only to the temptations Jesus encountered and the sins He gave His perfect life to save us from. Verse 2 is a transition from Jesus' victory in finishing sin to the call for Christian living in verse 3. Verse 2 is surely true of Christians. Those who know Christ should not give **the rest of** their **time in the flesh to the lusts of men, but to the will of God.** Some translations are carefully worded to make verse 2 apply to Christians rather than to Christ: "Therefore, since Christ suffered in the flesh, arm yourselves also with the same resolve—because the One who suffered in the flesh has finished with sin—in order to live the remaining time in the flesh, no longer for human desires, but for God's will" (vv. 1-2, HCSB).

Jesus is more than our example; He is our Savior and Lord. His presence within us motivates us and empowers us to follow His example. The example in verses 1-2 is His overcoming temptation and putting priority on doing **the will of God.** This is clear in verse 3: "For there has already been enough time spent in doing the will of the pagans: carrying on in unrestrained behavior, evil desires, drunkenness, orgies, carousing, and lawless idolatry" (HCSB).

What are the lasting lessons in 1 Peter 4:1-3?

1. Christ suffered for us in the days of His flesh.

2. By overcoming temptation and atoning for sin, Jesus Christ finished with sin.

3. The risen Christ enables believers to finish with sin and replace slavery to human desires with doing God's will.

4. The sins of the past should be past.

Count It a Privilege to Suffer for Christ (1 Pet. 4:12-16)

*Was Peter writing about future or present trials? In what sense were the trials **fiery**? How will **sufferings** give way to **joy**? What teaching of Jesus is reflected in these verses? What is the history of the title **Christian**?*

4:12-16: Beloved, think it not strange concerning the fiery trial which is to try you, as though some strange thing happened unto you: [13]but rejoice, inasmuch as ye are partakers of Christ's sufferings; that, when his glory shall be revealed, ye may be glad also with exceeding joy. [14]If ye be reproached for the name of Christ, happy are ye; for the spirit of glory and of God resteth upon you: on their part he is evil spoken of, but on your part he is glorified. [15]But let none of you suffer as a murderer, or as a thief, or as an evildoer, or as a busybody in other men's matters. [16]Yet if any man suffer as a Christian, let him not be ashamed; but let him glorify God on this behalf.

Some translations see verse 12 as a prediction of future persecutions that will involve literal fire (**the fiery trial which is to try you,** KJV). Other translations see this as a description of present persecutions, which are like the refining fire of 1:7: "Dear friends, do not be surprised at the painful trial you are suffering, as though something strange were happening to you" (NIV). Some interpreters see this as a situation similar to that in Hebrews. The readers had experienced many kinds of persecution, but no one had yet shed his blood (Heb. 10:32-34; 12:4). The Christians in Asia Minor had been slandered, but a more severe persecution lay ahead. Nero used fire in his persecution. History shows that a life-or-death persecution came to their area by the early second century. Therefore, many translators think Peter was focusing on their present trials. His words about suffering in verses 13-16 sound as if Peter were writing about persecutions they were already experiencing.

The word **fiery** is linked with the words **try you** ("test you," HCSB). This is the same idea taught in 1:7. The image is of the refiner's fire from which comes the gold.

Further, the readers should not be surprised as if suffering was **some strange thing.** After all, Jesus had faced opposition, and He had predicted similar trials for His followers. Instead of being surprised, they should **rejoice** because they were **partakers of Christ's sufferings.** Although they were suffering now, they also should remember that **when** Christ's **glory shall be revealed,** they would **be glad also with exceeding joy.** Present suffering is nothing compared to the future glory and joy.

Jesus' final Beatitude is reflected in the first part of verse 14. The two key words from this sentence are also found in Matthew 5:11: *makarioi* (**happy,** "blessed") and *oneidizo* (**reproached,** "revile"). Being reviled for Christ's sake means that **the spirit of glory and of God resteth upon you. Partakers of Christ's sufferings** enter into the experience of Christ's sufferings, not as adding to His saving work, but as sharing His self-giving spirit. And just as the humiliation of His suffering led to the glory of His exaltation (Phil. 2:5-11), so will those who identify with Him in His sufferings eventually share in His glory.

In verse 15 Peter returned to one of his warnings against the terrible influence of Christians who deserve punishment because they are not innocent sufferers, as Christ was, but sinners and criminals. Peter mentioned two heinous crimes: being **a murderer** or **a thief. Evildoer** is a more general word for "any other kind of criminal" (NIV). **A busybody in other men's matters** is "a meddler" (NIV, HCSB). Concerning the word **busybody** Peter Davids wrote: "The word *allotriepiskopos* comes from two root words, *allotrios,* 'belonging to another,' and *episkopos,* 'overseer.' . . . It is probable that our author is concerned that Christians in their rejection of idolatry and pagan morality or their zeal for the gospel not put their noses (or worse) into situations in which they ought not to be involved."[4]

The title **Christian** had its origin in Antioch (Acts 11:26). It means "a partisan of Christ" and may have been intended originally as a term of derision. It is found only two other times in the New Testament—each time in a negative way. Herod Agrippa II used the word when he rejected Paul's invitation to believe (Acts 26:28). Peter used it here to describe the hostility of the people that resulted in Christians suffering for bearing that name.

What are the lasting lessons in 1 Peter 4:12-16?

1. Christians should not be surprised when they are persecuted.

2. When they are persecuted, Christians identify themselves with the sufferings of Christ.

3. Persecuted Christians should rejoice because they will share Christ's glory.

4. No Christian should be ashamed of suffering because of being a Christian.

Trust God and Do Right (1 Pet. 4:19)

*How can you tell if your suffering is **according to the will of God**? What two responses should you make if it is?*

4:19: Wherefore let them that suffer according to the will of God commit the keeping of their souls to him in well-doing, as unto a faithful Creator.

The world is filled with suffering people. Some are suffering for doing wrong. In verse 15 Peter warned against suffering of this kind. Such suffering is not an expression of God's will in the sense referred to in verse 19. Here Peter had in mind the kind of suffering he had been commending—suffering for righteousness' sake. Suffering because you are a Christian is to **suffer according to the will of God.** This does not mean that suffering pleases God but that God is pleased by faithfulness and courage. Lots of suffering is in neither of these two categories. It is the kind of suffering that comes from living in an imperfect world. God seldom explains why a godly person suffers, but He does assure us that He is at work to bring good out of evil (Rom. 8:28).

In suffering that is inflicted because of our faith and in unexplained suffering, Peter told the sufferers to do two things. He repeated the admonition to keep doing the right thing **(well-doing).** He also called on sufferers to **commit the keeping of their souls to** God, **as unto a faithful Creator. Commit** ("entrust," NASB, NRSV, HCSB) is the same word used by Jesus as He died: "Father, into thy hands I commend my spirit" (Luke 23:46). It is a term used for entrusting something valuable to a trustworthy person for safekeeping. The word **souls** here refers to all that a person has or is. Those who are persecuted for being Christians entrust themselves to the Lord in life and in death.

A young missionary journeyman returned from overseas duty. He would not tell others the name of the country in which he had served for two years. He wanted to protect the converts from Islam that he had met. Islamic law prescribes death for those who leave that religion. Although the government of that country wouldn't directly enforce this sentence, it would look the other way when family members carried it out.

Another convert from Islam was returning to his homeland. Christian friends were afraid for him and the persecution he would face. He replied, "No worry. Jesus will make me strong."

What are the lasting lessons in 1 Peter 4:19?

1. Suffering for Christ's sake is according to God's will in the sense that God wants His people to be faithful unto death.

2. Believers who suffer persecution should entrust themselves into the hands of the faithful God.

❖ Spiritual Transformations

Christians should always be ready to explain what they believe and why. Since Christ finished His mission of salvation, believers ought to leave past sins behind them. Christians should expect to be persecuted if they are faithful to Christ. Persecuted believers should entrust themselves to God, who is always faithful.

Fellow Christians in some other countries are enduring the worst forms of persecution. About all American believers confront is ridicule and misunderstanding.

If someone asked you why you are a Christian, what would you say?

_____

Are you ever ridiculed for being a Christian? How do you handle such ridicule? _____

Prayer of Commitment: Lord, give me the courage to speak and live for You in every situation. Amen.

[1]J. N. D. Kelly, *A Commentary on the Epistles of Peter and of Jude*, in Harper New Testament Commentaries [Peabody, Massachusetts: Hendrickson Publishers, 1988], 140.
[2]Wuest, *First Peter*, 88.
[3]Kelly, *Epistles of Peter and of Jude*, 168.
[4]Davids, *The First Epistle of Peter*, 169.